SOFTWARE PORTABILITY

To Sue, James, Robert and Jane

Software Portability

John Henderson MSc, JP, MA, FBCS, FRSA

Senior Research Fellow,
Department of Computing
King's College London (KQC)

Gower Technical Press

Published by
Gower Technical Press Ltd,   Gower Publishing Company,
Gower House,   Old Post Road,
Croft Road,   Brookfield,
Aldershot,   Vermont 05036,
Hants   GU11 3HR,   U.S.A.
England

British Library Cataloguing in Publication Data
Henderson, John
    Software portability.
    1. Computer systems. Software. Portability
    I. Title
    005.3

Library of Congress Cataloging-in-Publication Data
Henderson, John, M.Sc.
    Software portability / John Henderson.
        p.   cm.
    1. Software compatibility.   I. Title.
    QA76.6.H458 1988
    005—dc19 88-4789

ISBN 0 291 39730 1

Typeset from disk by Textflow Services Ltd, Belfast
Printed and bound in Great Britain by
Anchor Brendon Ltd, Tiptree, Essex

Contents

Preface

This book is about software portability. This is a subject which has received surprisingly little analysis. There is a great deal of talk about how the use of this operating system or that language will make programs portable and thus extend their usefulness to the user. There is little discussion about what defines portability, and how it is to be achieved.

There are not many books about the subject, and much of the published material in articles addresses itself to particular ways of making certain classes of program portable. However, there is much to be gained from such material and this book contains suggestions for further reading.

It was suggested to me that a book on the subject might be of interest and within my abilities. The research undertaken led me to a position I had not anticipated. I had rather naively assumed that with the increasing use of high-level languages programs were no longer so highly machine-dependent as they had been and that software written using high-level languages was relatively easily portable. I found this was not the case. Accordingly, I set out to identify the problems that prevented programs being readily moved from one system to another and find ways of overcoming them. My own company had a contract to support a large program for a client and to make it available to any authorized user with a FORTRAN compiler. We also had an in-house modelling package which we wanted to be able to sell and support widely. I looked at these programs and discovered that the two groups in the company had developed rather different strategies, both of which allowed the programs to be transported.

In my group, I had myself developed an ALGOL 60 compiler and run-time library which was intended to allow the migration of ALGOL 60 programs from one particular computer to another. This had given me some insight into the problems which arise from the interpretation of standards and which can arise from the addition of external function libraries! I also implemented an operating system which provided a portability route for applications programs at source code level and supported by emulation load-module level portability for another system.

I was very fortunate that I was able to call on the expertise of a variety of individuals each of whom was involved in some aspect of portabilty, and this gave me a much wider appreciation of ways to solve the problem.

What I failed to do was to pin down the causes of the incompatibilities and inconsistencies which cause so much of the difficulty. I don't know if the cause is pride, ignorance or incomprehension on my part. Yet I believe that at the root of the problem lies a multitude of inconsistent man-made decisions.

I hope that the book will serve a variety of purposes. First, it should convince the reader that there is a real problem importing software. The reason that programs do not transport easily is not because they are badly or carelessly written. It takes considerable extra effort to make them transportable. It is necessary to develop a strategy for this. Next the reader should examine claims made by sellers of panaceas with rather more insight and so be able to evaluate these products more effectively. The third thing a general reader should learn is that there is a range of solutions to the problem and that each has an associated cost and so he should be able to assess the economics of the alternative approach he may adopt.

A reader faced with the problems of designing and implementing portable software will be made aware of the different technical approaches that can be adopted. He should then be able to choose the appropriate solution and have at least some signposts to the realization of that solution.

During the relatively long time that the book has been in the course of preparation, I have constantly expected to have been overtaken by events, so that the message would be a simple one, 'use language "X" and you will have portable programs'. This has not happened and the proliferation of 'solutions' and their versions and the different implementations have continued. This means that the designer and programmer have still to do their own work to produce portable code.

To start with the book presents an analysis of why portability is a problem. It then suggests the possible solutions in three main categories, and indicates the advantages and costs of these three approaches. This consideration of the possible avenues that can be taken helps clarify the issues and provides some insight into competing claims for portability and shows a program designer where the problems exist.

The second chapter presents a discussion of the causes of these problems including those induced by the hardware designs. In this chapter the reader is shown at least some of the ways in which design decisions in the hardware affect the execution of programs and the portability of data.

In Chapter 3 there is a review of the problems which occur in the design and implementation of software on that hardware. This chapter shows how different designers of systems software make choices which militate against easy portability.

Chapter 4 identifies three distinct mechanisms to achieve portability. There is a discussion of what is involved in taking each of these routes and of the circumstances which guide the choices to be made.

The three approaches are then examined in some detail. First consider the 'ground-up' systems. These are complete environments of operating system, languages, tools and applications. The various ways of developing such systems are considered.

In Chapter 6 we look at emulation. There are circumstances when the only practical approach to preserve the use of a program is by emulating its original environment. The problems of and solutions to such emulations are discussed.

The final approach described in Chapter 7 is the 'symbiotic' system, one designed to fit comfortably into a wide variety of environments with minimum demands made on that environment. This is perhaps the realistic approach for all but the largest and most ambitious suppliers of programs. Guidelines sketching various ways of identifying and avoiding pitfalls are given.

The literature which seriously discusses portability issues is sparse but one area that has received rather more coverage is compiler portability. Chapter 8 is devoted to a discussion of this topic, not in the anticipation that many readers will rush out and build portable compilers but because the presentation will give insight into the problems faced, and some of the techniques which are used to overcome these. Such techniques may prove to be of wider application.

The solution to portability is often mistakenly seen as the choice of the right language. In Chapter 9 I review the available candidates and indicate criteria for choice. This naturally leads to somewhat disappointing conclusions, because it is apparent that languages take a long time to become established, widely available and reasonably consistently implemented.

A more encouraging chapter discusses a variety of software tools, which can either be found already in existence or which would repay building by the implementor.

The final chapter reviews the successful techniques and discusses the possible effects of future trends.

As I stated earlier I am not in a position to offer a panacea for creating portable software. Yet I consider it essential that a system builder who is considering development of (portable) software must take a strategic viewpoint as to what and how much portability he is likely to achieve. If by reading this book he is better prepared to face this vital task then I would feel rewarded and the book has been worth the toil.

John Henderson

Acknowledgements

Thanks are due to Brian Shearing, Martyn Jeffreys and John Wootton for their help, advice and support.

Introduction

This book is intended to give an overview of many aspects of software portability. It is easier to say what it is not intended to achieve than to give a succinct account of its goals.

At the end of it a reader should have a good idea of where the problem arises and an outline of the various approaches that can be adopted to alleviate the problem.

A prospective buyer of a 'portable' solution might have developed enough insight to examine more closely the claims of the vendor and be able to gauge for himself how the various problems have been overcome.

A software writer will be able to choose from a variety of approaches and have some idea of the technical costs. To choose a route to achieving portability implies making economic decisions. There is a price to be paid in the sort of facilities the program offers, the mechanisms to be devised for controlling its writing and maintenance and the additional testing that will be required.

The real problem about portability is that the problem should not exist. There are no very good technical reasons why there is such a divergence of techniques. Equally, while all cars have their pedals arranged in the same order, light switches can vary between different models in the same manufacturer's range. Arguments can be advanced to justify any decision; certainly a case can be made for the rich variety of programming environments and languages available. However, the brake pedal is in the same place whether it is controlling a cable-operated drum-brake or servo-assisted hydraulic discs with anti-lock electronics. To stop the car you press the same pedal.

Equally the problem is not one amenable to an intellectual solution. No new program design methodology or a new programming paradigm will cope with human perversity about what to do with the most significant bit when 7-bit ASCII is stored in an 8-bit byte!

This book does not purport to be comprehensive. There is no way that all successful approaches to producing portable programs could be presented, discussed and analysed. Even if today it were true that the survey in the book was truly exhaustive, tomorrow some new approach would invalidate the claim.

What it does do however is show that the problem has many aspects. Rather than accept that 'UNIX' or 'C' is the answer, it shows that there are problems to be overcome which such solutions may assist, but that the solution remains firmly in the hands of the program designer and implementor who cannot abdicate his responsiblity to a systems programmer elsewhere.

Another aspect of portability to be considered is the cost in terms of delivered facilities. A program using MS/DOS in a 'responsible' way will have slower screen response than one which bypasses the operating system and writes directly to the screen buffer. It is entirely reasonable to pay for something desirable, it is important to realize that a price is being paid and what that price is.

There are books which explain in great detail how to write 'Portable FORTRAN'; this book does not attempt to provide a set of rules. It would be impossible, for the target is moving. C is currently the subject of standardization, and not until such a standard is promulgated and all compilers adhere can the rules be enunciated. The FORTRAN target has moved; the urge to improve, or should that be 'meddle', seems unstoppable. Only by grasping the principles involved can a designer decide for himself how to control his own project.

Implied in the book is the idea of designing and implementing a run-time support environment which provides consistent facilities to all programs using it and which can be reliably and consistently implemented on all hosts. It might seem attractive to present such an environment as a model or suggestion. A comprehensive solution would be large and unlikely to be tailored adequately to an individual set of problems. It is called an operating system, it provides solutions to all problems and is quite comprehensive. However, it is large and difficult to implement and maintain; what is suggested is that the basic principle be considered and, if felt appropriate, a minimal sub-set of features incorporated.

Portability and the future

The problems preventing the goal of easy portability are well known. The solutions are less well understood. What discernible trends emerge to give hope for the future? There is no discernible trend towards hardware standardization. Each manufacturer continues to produce his own idiosyncratic ideas. Certainly the trend of order code design is towards multi-register, stack-oriented architectures, but without compatibility between manufacturers. Compatibility by manufacturers with their own previous hardware is a noticeable trend and obviously to be welcomed. This is apparent only in minis and mainframes. The problems of designing 16-bit micros are currently too great to incorporate compatibility on chip; the solution being adopted at the micro end of the market is the incorporation of additional processors. This is economically justified and will presumably continue. The main hurdles still lie in the software. It is still the case that a manufacturer offers incompatible systems on the same hardware, and that independently supplied implementations of the same standard are not totally compatible. The emergence of single sources of compilers and operating systems for different hardware is likely to lead to a great degree of compatibility. However, that route tends to tie the user to one supplier.

Software standards have two associated problems. First, despite strenuous efforts to remove ambiguities and ensure a complete specification, differences in implementations always arise. Second, standards may inhibit innovation. It would be desirable for floating point to be provided to a standard format and accuracy. It would be nice if there were consistency in the use of the 8th bit in ASCII characters. However, the best hope for future portability seems to lie in emulation and support of existing *de facto* standards embedded in new systems. Certain operating systems, from the plethora available, have achieved and are achieving a high degree of acceptance and use, and while they demonstrably do not represent the ultimate in design or facilities, they are and will be widely used.

If the designers of new systems can accept the lessons of the past and incorporate – as is certainly technically possible – support for these popular systems in their new designs, then perhaps there can be an orderly transition to the new and not a cataclysmic upheaval. Current designs have improved to the point at which it is reasonable to expect their facilities to be at least a subset of future designs. Surely some sort of tree-structured directories for filing systems will be implemented.

The two hurdles that stand in the way of this path are software protection and technical arrogance. The owner of a popular and widely used program will quite naturally want to retain his rights and ownership in it, and unless he can profit from his ideas, he is very unlikely to make the investment necessary for the initial success. However, the situation is unclear about where his ownership lies, and an equitable and clear legal position accepted internationally would reduce uncertainties in this area. Second, systems programmers are not as a breed as willing to learn from others as perhaps they should be. The temptation to improve is strong. The question is sometimes, shall I get it right this time, or shall I maintain compatibility?

Problems and successes in portable programming

Moving working programs between different computers and systems has been an expensive chore for most of the history of computing. The problems exist both for the computer user looking to improve and upgrade his computing facilities, while protecting his existing investment in programs and data, and for the software supplier seeking to reach as wide a market for his products as possible. The light at the end of the tunnel has been sighted apparently several times. This book examines the current situation and presents some guidelines.

1

Overview of portable software

1

Overview of portable software

'Take what you want and pay for it' said God

Wouldn't it be nice if all programs ran on all computers? Nice for the suppliers – they could reach a far wider market; nice for the users – they would have the widest possible choice of programs. However the world is not like that – nor will it be. It is questionable how nice it would be to inhabit such a world. No program could then be written to avail itself of the new features of manufacturer X's latest technological breakthrough, so machine design would stagnate and, hectic and erratic though the change in computing has been over the last 30 years, the end user has benefited and will continue to benefit from improvements in price and performance. Hardware prices have dropped, bringing computers and computing into fields unthinkable 10 years ago. 'Space Invaders' and 'Simon' may not have the gravitas of a model of the economy – but they are more fun and much more widely available. Children are learning readily at school what for some of us were hard-earned and scarce skills.

However, it would be equally disastrous to return to the times when a manufacturer announced a new computer and his customers threw away all their working programs and started writing them again from scratch in Assembler. Between these extremes there must be a middle way which allows a wide choice, avoids re-inventing wheels and yet allows the state of the art to advance. So what should the goals of portable software be?

Let's consider who could benefit and whether these benefits to different groups of people are reconcilable. First the user: by definition the user has a reasonable amount of software the running of which is of importance to him. Whether this user has a large batch mainframe, a time sharing mini or a micro, as a user he has an investment in programs which he has written, bought or laboriously typed in from a page or two of densely printed Hex codes in his monthly magazine. Techniques which allow that user to improve his hardware and retain the use of all those programs are obviously of great benefit.

Second software suppliers. Increasingly users want to buy packages, i.e. ready written and working programs. So software suppliers are tending to produce packages. These are expensive to produce and there are considerable benefits to the supplier if he can extend the range of computers on which his programs will run and which will allow him to offer packages quickly on the latest 27-bit micro to hit the market.

Third, manufacturers, whose interest is somewhat different. They want to get new customers and then keep them – computer manufacturers get a good proportion of their business by selling both upgrades and additional new machines to their existing customers. They also need to provide a wide range of software on their systems. To lure new customers away from other manufacturers, ideally they should be able to run existing programs, but ensure new ones can't emigrate – except on their own new machine. The ubiquitous micro has reduced the differences between the offerings at the low price end of the market and manufacturers then must compete on price and packaging, service and reliability and hope to gain the loyalty of their customers that way.

Techniques for producing portable software have been largely developed in university departments. A few individuals have achieved considerable success in their efforts and some of these techniques will be discussed in later chapters. However, it is commercial pressures that are the main driving force behind what is happening in the world of computing and before proceeding to the chapters discussing various topics in detail perhaps we can look briefly at those changes that are relevant to portability.

Recent changes and portability

Most computers now in use are based on microprocessors, and, while many 8-bit micro chips were designed and marketed, considerable success in terms of volume sales has been achieved by only a few models. The Intel 8080 and the Zilog Z80, the latter design having an order code which is a superset of the former, have been widely used and are the foundation for the success of CP/M. This in turn has opened up a market for independent suppliers of software whose products will run on CP/M – 8080/Z80 micros. The Motorola 6502 has achieved success both in the Apple and Acorn BBC systems. Those each have their own different operating systems. However, their widespread acceptance means there exists a significant software market for products based on these machines. A fascinating development is the availability of CP/M for an Apple. This is achieved by hardware. The hardware option contains a Z80 micro and thus the compatability is achieved by introducing a second CPU. Of course a second CPU runs more quickly than an emulator program could, ensures compatibility, but is actually cheaper. The reduction in price of hardware has opened up an avenue for portability by introducing hardware techniques, rather than software, economically.

Sixteen-bit micros are now becoming much more widely available. These micros fall into two main categories: those which allow the user access to a large address space; and those restricting him to 64K bytes. This latter group may have software mechanisms to address a larger space but each program, at any given instant, is restricted to 64KB. The former allows, in principle, virtually unlimited space, but in practice a program will be restricted to a subset of the entire address space. So far no clear winner has emerged. The original IBM personal computer used a derivative of the Intel 8086, subsequent models have used more powerful but compatible processors. UNIX-like systems are available for both the Zilog Z8000 and the Motorola 68000.

Strangely, order code compatibility with previous chips has not weighed heavily in these designs and at least one 16-bit processor system on the market also incorporates a separate 8-bit processor to allow the running of existing programs. The provision of facilities to run existing programs on new systems by incorporating additional hardware is becoming widespread across the entire spectrum of system sizes and prices.

It is perhaps the most cost-effective route away from being tied to a particular order code whose relative disadvantages are becoming apparent, but in which there is a considerable software investment.

It would seem that the high hopes held out for portable software for many years have been somewhat disappointed. The mechanisms that are in use are not necessarily those expected. Despite years of academic criticism

FORTRAN and COBOL are widely used still. BASIC, with all its widely known defects, is still very popular. New languages with all the inevitable problems that they bring are being designed. Each one is promised as at least one answer to most if not quite all of life's problems.

One final and fascinating effect of the proliferation of similar machines is the issue of software protection. Much effort is applied to ensuring that programs, while being available readily, are restricted so that only the original purchaser can use them.

The aim of this book is to consider the problems that must be recognized and overcome if portable software is to be achieved and so the discussion is aimed to a large extent at designers and writers of software. It addresses itself in general to the larger and more complex pieces of software and regards portability as meaning something more than being able to run a program on more than one manufac- turer's CP/M micro or IBM clone. Accordingly various machine architectures are considered and a fairly wide range of languages and operating systems is looked at. The examples in Chapter 9 illustrate problems overcome using FORTRAN. The problems with other languages will be at least similar, and FORTRAN is probably more widely available than anything else. BASIC is discussed but it has significant limitations both in execution speed and facil- ities, which make it unsuitable for many larger applica- tions. It may be that total portability, i.e. recompiling/ loading a program – without any changes – on to a new machine, and that new version running without error is possible, but its performance may well be inadequate. Perhaps the best solution is to ensure that the areas of potential problems are isolated to well defined sections of the program so that only these need change. Thus the extent of the problem of transporting a particular program can be known and controlled.

So what is portable software? It is software that can run

on at least two different machines with minimal changes. The extent of change needed as a proportion of total effort to rewrite is one measure of portability. What are different machines? Are two different models of the same range different machines? Is the same machine with a different operating system a different machine? Certainly both these cases can cause problems and prevent programs running identically on each or at all. Is it the ability to run the same binary image (i.e. the compiled and loaded image) on different machines? Even if the two machines have different instructions sets, this can be achieved. Or is a program or set of programs to which some largely mechanical processing is applied which produces versions of programs which can thus be run on two machines, portable? However, what is important is that the execution of the software on its various host machines should produce identical results from identical data.

What sorts of programs are transported? Historically much effort has been put into compiler portability. There are good reasons for this. First, it helps applications portability if identical compilers (i.e. compilers which accept identical syntax and produce identical results from the same source code) are widely available. Second, when a new computer is produced, the sooner its necessary support software can be produced the better, and what better than to import working compilers? Third, compilers have traditionally been the most widely available software packages. Users may have their own ideas about applications, but they want standard compilers for the languages they use and have used before.

Compilers were probably the first software that users expected to be available packaged 'off the shelf'. Manufacturers might supply compilers for only a few languages themselves and thus actively encourage independent suppliers to extend that range. Therefore effort was put into developing techniques for transportable compilers.

One problem historically is that compilers are evaluated for speed of compilation, and for the quality of the code produced which affects the speed of execution of the program. These factors imply a considerable need to tailor the compiler closely to the target hardware. Proof that this pressure still exists can be derived from the availability of BASIC and Pascal compilers for computers which already have interpretive or semi-interpretive systems available.

Operating systems are only now becoming widely available from third-party suppliers and thus for the first time there is interest and pressure to use portability techniques in their implementation for commercial use. By their nature as the ultimate manipulators of the hardware it is necessary that some elements at least are written in a machine-dependent manner. Efficiency, which is crucial in operating systems, requires a significant degree of tailoring, in particular of input/output routines.

Applications programs have traditionally been written for specific users to their particular specifications. As the price of the hardware has plummeted and the productivity of programmers has remained fairly static, the cost of bespoke software becomes an increasingly high proportion of the total systems price. Thus there is a growing trend to the purchase of standard packages. In this case the supplier hopes to recoup his investment from several sales and make his profit from many. Accordingly the wider his market the better and the greater will be his efforts to achieve portability.

One requirement still obtains. It is necessary that the program executes acceptably quickly. There is no longer a requirement for programmers, in general, to spend so much time on hand-optimizing programs and making them as small or as fast as possible. Nevertheless it is essential that the program execution speed is acceptable. The disadvantages of interpretation for example are highlighted by the degree of interest by home computer users in machine code. It is useless in practice to transport a program if no-one can be bothered to use it. Having said that, program efficiency is in general best achieved by algorithmic design and by paying attention to the overheads of input/output. Effort spent on algorithmic design is unlikely to interact adversely with portability methods. Unfortunately input/output tends to be a main area of difference between most systems. The differences lie between what facilities are available, how the facilities are accessed and how effectively they are implemented. Thus it may be possible to transport a working program quite easily to a new machine only to find that its performance is unacceptable.

2

Hardware problems

2

Hardware problems

For a program to be truly portable it must execute on at least two different machines. In what repects then do machines differ? Differences may be major or minor, but all differences must be accounted for to ensure portability. First, let's look at major intrinsic differences between computers – in instruction codes and data representation.

Instruction sets

Instruction sets may differ considerably but this may not necessarily be significant. Each individual set has different ways of performing various operations but the same effects can be achieved in them all.

Data representation

In data representation, the most important feature is in the representation of numerical data. Computers are available with the built-in ability to perform arithmetic operations on at least three different representations of numeric data. These are integer, real and decimal.

Integer arithmetic
It is reasonable to assume that any current computer will have the ability to add and subtract some representation of integer numbers. However the particular representation used is important. There is a strong move towards designing computers whose architecture is based on an 8 bit byte. The simpler micros operate on 8-bit numbers; more complex machines will operate on 16-bit numbers, 32-, 36- or 48- or even 60-bit numbers. The number of bits determines the range of numbers that may be represented – 8 bits allow 256 unique patterns, 16 bits 65 536 patterns, in general $2n$ (where n is the number of bits) patterns. The mapping of these unique patterns into numeric values is arbitrary, but it is convenient to regard the 'right-hand' bit as the low-order bit and associate each bit moving left as the next higher order. Thus we have a more or less universal convention for representing positive numbers.

However there are two widely used conventions for the representation of negative numbers. These are 'one's complement' and 'two's complement'. A feature of both ways of representing negative numbers is that the high-order bit now assumes the significance of a sign bit. Two's complement means that 8-bit bytes can represent numbers in the range of -128 to $+127$. In one's complement the range -127 to $+127$ can be held. In this representation there is 'negative zero' i.e. all one bits representing zero as well as all zero bits. It is also desirable that the hardware produces an indication of arithmetic overflow and carry. This allows two things: the ability to perform 'multiple precision arithmetic' so that arithmetic representation of integers is not restricted to any arbitrary size by the inbuilt arithmetic hardware; and to detect numerical operations which produce erroneous results. There are no illegal patterns of bits in an integer implying an impossible number, as there might be with both decimal and real representations. Arithmetic operations can occur which produce erroneous answers but the resulting bit patterns are themselves quite legal. It is essential to check for such errors at the time they might occur, or be certain that none can occur. Unfortunately by no means all computers detect overflow, and few languages provide intrinsic facilities to programmers so that a program may check whether it has occurred. It is necessary therefore to carry out preliminary checks on the data to avoid errors which would otherwise be undetected.

Many computers now have instructions to perform multiple-length arithmetic operations and instructions for multiplication and division to be performed in hardware. Integer division is only fully defined where both divisor and dividend are positive, and different answers may be produced by different machines in the case of division using the same negative numbers.

Real arithmetic

Real or floating point numbers are represented differently from integers and there are many more variations in the formats used. A real number is represented in two parts, each of which may occupy several bytes. The components are the exponent and the mantissa. Each of these has a size and on the size of exponent depends the range of numbers that can be represented and on the size of mantissa the accuracy. There is also a requirement for one sign to be associated with the exponent and another with the mantissa. It is customary to provide both a single-precision real number representation, which is often 32 bits long, and a double precision which can take 48 or 64 bits. Sometimes not all the bits in the double precision case are used, so two different manufacturers' 48-bit numbers may well not both have the same accuracy. The use and layout of the bits is not standard, though standards for both representation and for manipulation have been proposed by the IEEE. Such differences in internal representation may well have an impact on the software needed to convert numbers into and out of character format. For portability of software and consistency of results real numbers present a significant problem. The problem of numerical significance may be further exacerbated by the actions of compilers which may change the sequence of arithmetic operations in the interests of efficiency but thereby reduce the accuracy of the results or even produce irrecoverable errors.

The differing internal representations will mean algorithmic differences in software which converts between strings of digits in character and real-number form. There is a further complication in that the provision of floating point hardware is not universal and so there could well be discrepancies between operations carried out by hardware and those by software floating point routines on the same machine. For example the 8087 co-processor, available for 8086 based systems, supports internally not only the IEEE standard representations but its own high-precision internal format for the preservation of precision. This could lead to differences in results.

Decimal arithmetic
The very early computers used in data processing operated on variable length strings of numerical data in which each digit was represented explicitly and separately. Some micros use similar schemes which implement decimal arithmetic. In these machines 4 bits are used to represent each digit. Only 10 of the possible 16 patterns are valid representations of digits. These 4-bit representations are not the same as the character representation in the various 6- or 8-bit codes. There is also a problem about the

representation of a negative sign for the number, which can be solved in various incompatible ways.

These arithmetic representations and manipulations must be well understood by the programmer seeking to write portable programs. This is largely because the computer implements the arithmetic in hardware and so there is no efficient solution available to the compiler designer seeking to provide consistency as he must use the instructions provided in hardware. Furthermore, some effort is needed to ensure consistency of results for a program which will use that inbuilt arithmetic. Care is also necessary to understand the conversion procedures between the various possible representations of data.

Character representation

So far we have discussed hardware features embedded deeply in the CPU architecture. The next topic – character representation – is also a hardware item, but is much more a convention, though a terminal might map byte to character image in hardware. To communicate between men and machines a set of symbols is used. This set of symbols is at least the alphabet (probably upper and lower case), the digits, punctuation marks, some arithmetic symbols and a few others. Some computers still operate on 6-bit characters, which restricts the number of unique symbols to 64, but most now use 8-bit bytes which allow theoretically 256 symbols. However this is many more than is needed for upper and lower case, digits and a wide set of punctuation marks – and so one of the main mapping conventions defines 128 symbols, including some non-printing. The mapping from a readable mark on paper to computer bit pattern is arbitrary, and so inevitably there are several incompatible systems. The most widely used is ASCII (American Standard for Code of Information Interchange) but EBCDIC (Extended Binary Coded Decimal Interchange Code) is also used (mostly by IBM) and they are different. Just to make life a little more interesting, there are even different punched card codes and paper tape codes. There are also systems with 6-bit codes. This is inadequate for many purposes, so shift and escape codes are defined to modify the interpretation of following codes thus allowing more symbols to be represented. This approach of course raises problems with the length of character strings as not all characters can be represented in a single 'byte', and so the length in bytes may not be the same as the length in characters.

Now the differences between the conventions are important for at least three reasons. The first and most trivial is that there may be minor differences between the symbols that each system is capable of representing. It is thus essential to ensure that all the characters used by a program, either in its data or its own representation, can be expressed in all of the possible conventions used by potential hosts.

A more important consideration is collating sequence. The mapping of symbols into bit patterns is arbitrary. However, inside the machine those patterns can be regarded as integers and manipulated as any other integers. The 8-bit number which is the character code for 1 is not necessarily the same as the 4-bit BCD (Binary Coded Decimal) for 1 or the 8 (or 16) integer for 1. However, for many applications it is convenient to be able to compare two characters, or two strings of characters, and to sort those characters or strings based on equality, greater than or less than relationships (e.g. alphabetical order). Indeed sorting of character strings, or searching for character strings, is a very important application area. But the results of these comparisons depend entirely on the convention in use – the computer compares only numbers. In the case of compilers, operating systems and other string processing requirements it is often necessary to be able to differentiate between alphabetic characters and digits. It cannot be assumed in all codes that the sequences A–Z and a–z are mapped into contiguous integers and so special care must be taken in even this simple task.

A third problem must be noted. While a character is stored as an 8-bit byte, the ASCII code defines only 7 bits; the 8th bit, which is the sign bit, can be and is used by different manufacturers in at least five different ways. It can always be set on, it can always be cleared or it can be used on a parity bit, and this in turn can be odd or even. In those four cases, any particular character is always represented by the same code. It is essential therefore to ensure the same convention is applied throughout any program or suite of programs using ASCII character data. Just to add to the confusion some word processing systems use the 8th bit for their own formatting conventions, and so the same character may not always have the same representation.

The collating sequence problems mentioned above are an obvious example of the sort of problem which results from using arithmetic mechanisms on what are essentially non-numeric data. Problems also arise when data compression techniques are used. Often it is necessary to operate on sets of information which do not have enough values fully to occupy a byte or word, whichever is the main addressable unit of storage. Obviously it is possible to waste the space not required, so that, for example, a logical variable which can take only one of two possible values, or again a flag indicating either male or female, requires only 1 bit but is often represented by a whole byte or word, the rest of which is put to no useful purpose. It is easier to do this than work out how to use each bit separately, but a price must be paid in memory utilization, in file storage and in data transfer times between memory and backing store. Depending very much on the size of the problem being solved it may become important to minimize the memory requirements and so pack the data as tightly as possible. There is a variety of techniques for reducing the storage requirement of text. Unfortunately packing and unpacking may again bring the programmer face to face with arithmetic operations and the use of the sign bit may produce undesirable effects.

One final point about machine idiosyncrasies which can cause problems is the naming of bits, bytes and words. Depending on the chosen convention the high-order bit of a 16-bit word may be numbered 0, 1, 15 or even 16. The equivalents for the low order bit are 15, 16, 0 and 1. Depending on the language in use and the conventional significance given to the bits in a word this can cause problems.

There are many machines which operate on bytes or words or both. On a word machine it is usual to store bytes thus:

$$
\begin{array}{ccc}
\text{byte n} & \text{byte n+1} & \\
0 & 1 & \text{word n}
\end{array}
$$

but it is possible to do it the other way round.

$$
\begin{array}{ccc}
\text{byte n+1} & \text{byte n} & \\
1 & 0 & \text{word n}
\end{array}
$$

It may be that words must have even addresses or that any byte can be the 'first' in a word. Words may be numbered consecutively and bytes not addressed directly at all.

This can be very confusing: one effect is that character pairs in strings can become reversed. This same problem shows itself in the way 16-bit addresses are stored in some 8-bit micros.

Data access

So far the discussion has covered problems in data representation and manipulation. There are also problems in data accessing mechanisms. The programmer can be shielded from some of these by software, but often hardware features do obtrude. One main restriction is total addressability. Many micros and minis are restricted to 64K bytes or, occasionally, words of logical space, that is to say only 16 bits can be used to specify an address so programs and their data must be restricted to that space; sometimes less as the system may itself occupy some of the same logical space. Software techniques are often provided to overcome this problem, but these are usually different from machine to machine. The techniques are normally not transparent to the user and impose conventions on the organization of both programs and data. The use of such techniques can also involve changes in the way the program is written. Increasingly machines provide what seems today practically unlimited addressability, though no doubt program sizes will grow to use it. If advantage is taken of these large address spaces, it will prove difficult to re-establish the necessary disciplines to move back to a smaller machine. Again some machines provide separate address spaces for instructions and data. Thus the traditional trade-off between program size and data area will not be possible – there are of course other potential benefits to be gained from such a separation. Finally, in the realms of large address spaces two main addressing mechanisms are employed. One presents the user with a large contiguous address space, the other with a set of many segments. The implications of these different approaches can impinge on program design and therefore portability.

Compatible machines

The final topic which must be taken into account is consideration of compatible machines or machine ranges.

Since the 1960s manufacturers have seen the advantages to themselves and their customers of offering a range of compatible computers, i.e. computers which implement the same instruction set, and which differ only in speed and price. There is a growing trend for third-party manufacturers to offer machines to compete with an existing supplier by offering the same instruction set. Thus the same instruction sets have been implemented many times by different people, quite possibly using different CPU implementation techniques and this can lead to incompatibilities. There are minor discrepancies between the implementation of the PDP/11 order code on different models. These differences are only to be found in the execution of rather subtle variations of the addressing modes and are unlikely to affect the average user.

A desirable feature increasingly available is hardware emulation where one processor exhibits the ability to execute the instructions of another – usually the predecessor in the manufacturer's range (e.g. PRIME 50 series, VAX, 2900 DME).

There is also the problem of optional extensions to an order code. In this case the user can choose to buy additional hardware to execute additional instruction types. Sometimes the design is such that the absence of the extra hardware causes a software emulation of the missing instruction to be used. Such options are less common now than once they were, with the exception of the provision of hardware floating point, which is still quite frequently an extra cost option. The position can thus arise where two machines nominally the same are in fact different in important details.

Differences do arise between the nominally identical: attempts are made to improve the execution of individual instructions, relative instruction speeds will alter, different implementations of the same order code are different, and minor differences will arise and may cause problems.

The areas so far discussed are concerned only with the intrinsic features of the CPU. The CPU is only one component of the total configuration. It determines the data representation internally and the set of instructions for manipulating it. On the configuration depends the mechanism for communicating with the world outside. This manifests itself in two different ways. One is exactly how the communication is effected and the other what communication is available.

There are two main I/O mechanisms. One is for the CPU to have special input/output instructions, the other is the so-called memory-mapped approach where certain memory addresses are reserved as device registers and where the computer uses its memory-referencing instructions to read and write these registers, which has the effect of performing I/O operations. The advantage of the second approach is that no special instructions need to be implemented but this is at the cost of reducing the logical address space available for a program.

In the first mechanism an I/O channel number has to be specified by the instruction driving a particular device. In the second the I/O register addresses can vary between configurations. This allows the channel number or the allocated register address to be allocated differently between similar configurations. Increasingly micros have a 'screen display area' in the total address space and this may not always be at the same address for machines nominally compatible.

So there is considerable scope for I/O configurations to vary significantly between computers that on the face of it are the same.

Equally, the devices connected to the configuration may well have quite different characteristics. Certainly different VDUs have different code sequences for cursor positioning and for invoking the increasingly powerful facilities provided.

If the disc packs are removable and are physically compatible there may be no easy way for one operating system to read a pack written by another. Disc drives differ in sector sizes, number of sectors and control protocols.

For magnetic tapes 0.5″ has become the standard width. However, there is more than one recording method and a wide range of possible recording densities and not all tape drives can read the full range of possible densities The parity convention chosen may be odd or even and the wrong parity can cause hardware-detected errors which make the tape unreadable.

Floppy discs come in various sizes, recording densities and sector allocation strategies and may not be an effective transportation medium. Audio cassette tapes used widely on home computers and smaller micros will almost certainly have different and incompatible techniques used on different manufacturers' systems or between different models from the same manufacturer.

3

Software problem areas

3

Software problem areas

For the purpose of this chapter, software is taken to mean support software and utilities, in contrast to applications programs. This definition includes operating systems compilers, loaders, editors etc.

The original aim of software was to simplify the programmer's task, to remove from him levels of detail and to provide mechanisms to translate from formal languages into machine code. From these origins grew the operating systems and compilers of today. A further benefit that became apparent was that as applications programs came to be written in standard languages remote from the details of a particular machine they could be run on other machines with appropriate compilers. So it seemed all that remained to guarantee that programs were portable was to ensure that standard compilers of well defined languages were available. Much effort has been put into producing language specifications and producing compiler verification systems. Yet programs are not always portable.

The problems lie in several areas. The first is progress and improvement. It became clear that the early languages were somewhat clumsy and deficient in features. This led to the design of a huge number of languages, most of which languish in decent obscurity. However it also led to the 'upgrading' of the successful languages. Desirable features were added in a fairly haphazard manner. Each manufacturer was able to point to the extras, and in general useful and desirable extras, his compilers offered. It started the incompatibility process. Old standard programs could be transported, newer ones could not. Hardware changed, the languages had been designed by people with experience of existing computers, and some features did not map easily on to the new systems.

As an example FORTRAN specifies that an integer and a single-precision real will each occupy one 'storage unit'. In 36-bit machines this makes sense; it wastes precious space and potentially wastes times in a 16-bit mini, and so is not implemented generally or consistently. Second, the problem is input/output (I/O). ALGOL 60 solved the problem neatly by ignoring it. All other languages had great problems defining it. Those that succeeded necessarily restricted I/O to that common to all systems. When I/O consisted of 80-column cards, magnetic tapes and printed paper, that wasn't too unacceptable, but interactive terminals and discs and the exciting possibilities they offered complicated the issue. The new facilities allow 'better' programs to be written, better in that they are faster, using for example random disc I/O, and better in that they have interactive data checking and execution.

There has been a strong trend to move away from batch to on-line working. All these problems and opportunities lead to the definition of new languages or to the addition of new facilities to existing languages. One problem remains, however. Language definition effort led to the development of syntactic description languages. The syntax of a language can be clearly and unambiguously defined. Its related semantics cannot. For a language to be widely available, it must have lots of implementations and, with every realistic effort made to avoid them, discrepancies nevertheless occur. The answer to that problem is to have one standard implementation, but economic considerations have ensured that for non-proprietary languages there are many implementations and for proprietary languages fewer installations. One minor point, which is still a nuisance, is language representation. A machine-readable program text from one machine may not be compilable by another. Silly details like the use of embedded 'tab' characters in programs or data or the representation of parentheses may foil portability. Lower case alphabetic characters are not available on all machines, and this can and does cause problems.

Language standards

Computer languages can be classified in as many ways as there are languages. Languages can be designed by an individual, or by a committee. They can be designed to incorporate mechanisms to handle all known problems, to handle a specific set of problems or to provide simple mechanisms from which further mechanisms can be built to handle more complex problems. They can be terse in their representation (e.g. APL) or they can be so verbose – to provide 'readability' – that programs have been written to expand relatively terse representations into full text before compilation. There are several COBOL generators available. Among the relatively few languages in common use, examples of each can be cited. Once a language has become widely accepted, there is a need for standards. Committees, preferably internationally recognized, are set up to produce definitive specifications. Two or more marginally different standards often appear. Deficiencies in the language become apparent and extensions and revisions are defined.

Sadly, perhaps, compilers have to be written by people and these compilers provide the ultimate definition of the language. What a compiler makes of a set of source text is the definition of this implementation of the language. Considerable efforts are made to tell the compiler writer what his compiler should do; considerable efforts are made to ensure that the compiler does just that. Nevertheless, it is what the compiler does do that provides the definition. Problems arise in several ways. First, some areas in the definition may be deliberately or accidentally left vague – these are to allow the compiler designer an opportunity to exercise his initiative. Second, some definitions are ambiguous and are interpreted differently by different people. Third, some implications of the language implementation may not have been anticipated by the language designers.

To try to cope with these problems two mechanisms at least have been adopted. These are verification programs, that is to say programs which check source code for syntactic correctness against the standard, and validation programs which are suites of programs designed to test features of the compiler and which should produce predictable results when compiled and run. It is important to check the compiler not only for its operation on correct programs, but also to see how effective it is at discovering errors and so suites of validation programs may include programs containing known errors.

Language definitions evolve. Deficiencies are rectified and improvements made. Over the last 20 years, ideas and techniques for writing programs have crystallized and improved and this has provided pressure for language improvement as well as for the design of new languages. It has been seen to be a good idea that languages should evolve, with certain fixed reference points. Whatever the merits of this approach, it leads inevitably to incompatibility.

There is one further aspect of compiler operation which can cause problems. This is optimization. For many years much effort has been made to ensure that the code produced by compilers compares adequately in both size and execution efficiency with good hand-written machine code. Before the economic priorities were changed, by computers becoming both faster and cheaper, acceptance of the use of high-level languages was restricted because of criticisms of comparative performance. The acceptance of the use of high-level languages is now virtually total, but old habits die hard. Compiler writers thus spend time and effort on designing generators to produce the best code possible. Optimizations can be made at various levels. It is possible to improve coding which is correct but which could have been written more efficiently, for example by removing the evaluation of constant expressions from inside loops and putting it outside so that it is executed only once, not once per iteration, or by realizing that multiplication by the induction (or controlled variable) of a loop can be reduced to a series of additions. In this sort of case the optimization makes changes that could have been made by the programmer to the original source text. This optimization improves coding techniques and is very unlikely to have any effect on the results of running the program.

The most difficult problem for the user is the optimization by compilers of arithmetic expressions. This can be restricted to a single statement or to a sequence of statements where execution is indivisible and so the sequence can be treated as a single statement. This optimization invariably involves the possibility of re-ordering the evaluation sequence and this can lead to arithmetic errors. A careful programmer will know the order of magnitude of his data items and can therefore so arrange the order of his evaluations to avoid overflow and retain maximum accuracy. Optimizations which change the order of calculations can nullify the benefits of all this effort and may therefore not only produce incorrect results on one machine, but results which vary between machines. Indeed two different compilers, or the use of various options of one compiler may produce different effects on the same machine.

Operating systems (O/S)

The main problems that software causes for portability lie not so much in the languages, even though problems remain in that area, but in the supporting operating systems. No software, except an operating system, intended to be easily portable will be expected to run on an 'empty' machine. Most suppliers of applications packages will expect their programs to co-exist with other applications, possibly from other sources, and use the manufacturer's operating system.

This is an area where there is considerable variety. What each operating system offers its users and how it achieves its goals vary. The divergence is considerable. The provision of operating systems is an area where manufacturers compete not only with each other, but with themselves. This internal competition proves, as nothing else could, that there is a strongly held belief that different approaches to computing and different classes of problem require different operating systems.

What sorts of operating systems are available and what facilities do they offer? The range is vast. The simplest are just ROM monitors, which sometimes include a BASIC interpreter, for a single-user micro. The most complex will supervise hundreds of user tasks and terminals, dozens of discs and other peripherals and several processors. The interface with the user varies widely; some are 'user friendly' and are intended for novice users, while the job control language on others is so complex that there are individuals employed exclusively as specialists in using them.

Operating systems can be single-user, multi-user, real-time, batch or a combination of the last three. Some multi-user systems are effectively multiple/single-user systems, while others allow one user to have many interacting tasks. Essentially operating systems conceal the details of the hardware from the user and define a meta-machine which has features not provided directly by the underlying hardware. It is via the operating system that the program has access to the peripherals and the clock. How the O/S does its housekeeping and scheduling has much less impact on the user than what is offered in terms of facilities. How it performs its various operations may well affect performance.

What then are these services? One of the first to consider is peripheral handling. Programs need to read input data, write output data and possibly produce and modify working files. Input can be from a terminal, a card reader, a file produced by another program, a magnetic tape, or from something unusual like a digitizer. Output can be to a terminal, a printer, a file, a plotter or communications line or TV screen, or something more exotic. Intermediate files, that is those files which the program produces for its own benefit, can be on tape or disc.

What sorts of disc files can be provided by the operating system and what features do they have? At the simplest level the O/S may allow the program unrestricted access to a physical disc drive, i.e. the program can read and write any sector on that disc. The next level up will allow access of a similar unstructured nature to a particular area of the disc (say one or more contiguous tracks). The next higher level names contiguous areas and the program has to 'open' the file, that is request the operating system to associate the name with the disc area and map his accesses to the appropriate area. The first two approaches do not involve named files; systems supporting such accesses do exist and there can be significant problems in avoiding conflicting accesses, where there is more than one user. More and more operating systems support named files and allow pseudo-direct access either not at all or as a special option. Mechanisms are also provided to prevent inter-user conflicts.

Once the concept of named files is introduced potential incompatibilities emerge. First, the name itself. Here there are two problems: first, how many characters in a name; second, which characters are legal. In some cases a language compiler may restrict the user to a greater extent than the system does, in that the language may implement only a subset of the names implemented by the system.

Names of files may be 6, 8, 32 or more characters in length. A commonly implemented naming convention is to divide the name into two parts, the second of which is called an extension (or type) often 3 characters long, which the operating system may use in accordance with some convention or other. The operating system may associate a version number with a file, automatically saving an old version when a new one is written.

The operating system may or may not support mechanisms for grouping files together into user (or sub-) directories. If it does it may or may not allow lower-level directories. Once at least one level of user directory is supported, then mechanisms will have to be provided to access files in more than one directory. There may also be mechanisms for controlling access both to other directories and to individual files; there may be directory pass-word protections; there may be file protection mechanisms. Some systems allow files to be flagged as read only, read–write, undeletable, etc.

Once a system supports named files, it must also

support disc allocation mechanisms. Some systems support fixed length files, the length of which is fixed when the file is created, so that when the file is created it must be large enough to hold all the data it will ever need to. Other systems will allocate file space on demand.

Systems allocating space on demand may impose quotas on users. Some will allow a space reservation in advance. If a program exceeds its quota, the entire disc or its fixed allocation, does the operating system detect the condition, does it provide mechanisms allowing the program to take corrective action or does it just 'blow up'?

How does a program access a file? The process of opening a file usually involves associating a unique descriptor with the file, e.g. a logical unit number (LUN) which is used in subsequent file-accessing operating. Most systems have an arbitrary limit to the number of open files at any given instant – say 16 or 256. Does the system supply the LUN, or does the user specify it? Are certain unit numbers used conventionally; is unit 6 always the printer, for example? Systems vary in which conventions they use. Once a file is 'open', can it be opened again by the same or some other user?

How can the data in the file be accessed? The most common access methods are sequential or direct access. Some operating systems implement keyed access as well. If it is sequential access can the program access arbitrarily sized records or is a block structure imposed? If it is direct access is a block structure imposed by the system? If it is direct access are 'holes' permitted or must all records up to the maximum be present?

Is it possible to access a direct access file sequentially or only by direct reference to records? Can a sequential file be accessed also by record number or displacement?

Some systems impose internal conventions on the data stored. How for example are ASCII data stored and how are ends of line denoted? Are packing techniques employed on character data? Is this information documented?

These are just some of the differences between operating systems' file systems.

Magnetic tapes are used less widely than previously by applications programs and are quite often used only for systems archiving. However, when available they are in many ways the best medium for data transfer between systems, for example transporting the programs themselves. Variations can occur in three possible areas. The first is physical – density and parity. The next two are software-related. Some systems use 'labelled' tapes and will reject outright tapes without acceptable logical labels. Once the tape has been accepted by the system there can be differences in block size, whether record lengths are fixed or variable, line terminators and character codes.

Floppy discs are also used as a transportable medium and even if the hardware is compatible differences arise in software in the interleaving algorithm chosen. Because floppy discs are slow, it is important that logically adjacent sectors of information are not physically adjacent. This sort of arrangement can reduce delays by positioning the first logical sector on the next track in such a way that the head movement time and rotational time are the same, so that when the head mechanism has moved to that track there is a good chance that it will not have to wait a complete revolution for the data (see Figure 3.1). The algorithms for such optimization vary between systems. Terminal accessing can impact software in two ways. The more intelligent terminals have facilities which are controlled by special command characters or strings, which are usually sequences of two or more characters. These command sequences vary between terminal types and so in order to support different terminal protocols the program must have these command sequences as data. Command sequences, whether sent or received, may con-

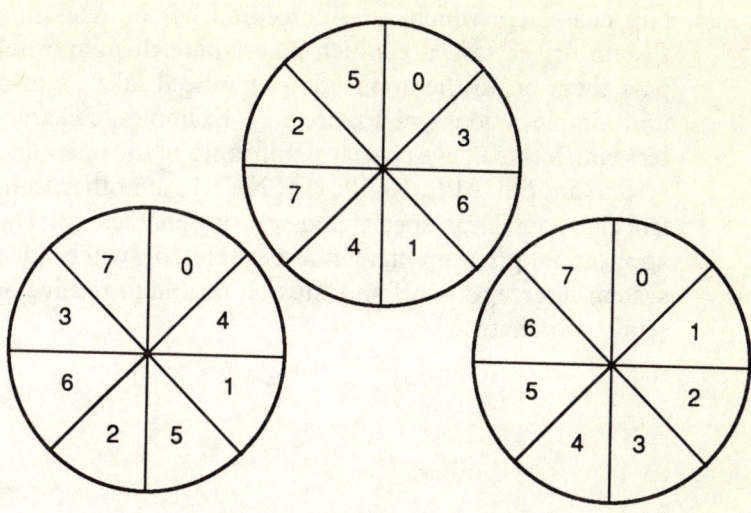

Figure 3.1   Possible logical organizations of floppy disc sectors.

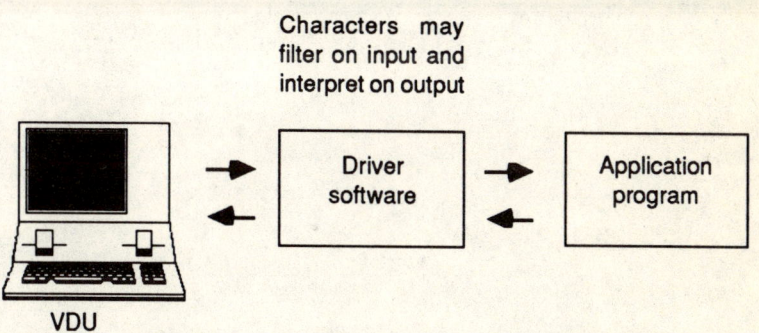

Figure 3.2   Interrelation between terminal–driver–application.

tain characters which are intercepted by the operating system driver software which may ignore them and not pass them on to the application or indeed take its own undesirable actions (see Figure 3.2). Examples of characters which often have special significance to the operating system are ESCAPE, RUBOUT, NULL and other 'control characters' (i.e. special non-printing characters). The application program may not be able to switch such system interception off and thus be unable to receive or send such characters.

4

Approaches to portability

4

Approaches to portability

We have seen in the previous chapters that there are good reasons why the production of portable software is not easy. There are many more problems to be overcome than can be solved merely by writing a program in a 'standard language'. It is of course one of the prerequisites when intending to write a portable program that a standard language be used. Some of the problems involved in such an approach will be covered in a later chapter.

It is essential to design the program right from the start with portability in mind. This will have advantages over and above the achievement of portability. It must surely be the case that any program intended to be portable will be expected to be widely used over a long time-frame. Portable programs are not intended to be thrown away. Thus a portable program will have not only to be designed for portability but also to be as correct as possible and capable of easy maintenance and enhancement. It will have to be good software. That is to say it must work, be acceptably efficient and contain as few bugs as possible. Thus it will need careful design *ab initio* and many of the criteria for portability will enforce a careful consideration of correct design.

There are three main classes of solution adopted to solve the portability problem. These are:

1   the 'ground-up' approach
2   the 'symbiotic' approach; and
3   the 'accommodating host'.

First, 'ground-up'. This is the solution exemplified by, amongst others, Micro COBOL and BOS and by C and UNIX. This approach provides a consistent set of facilities to produce a complete environment. The whole system – utilities, applications, compilers, filing system, device handlers – will be available on different computers. Of its nature this approach implies a vast volume of software that needs to be transported.

Second, 'symbiosis'. This approach is where the portable program has to live happily in whatever host environment is available. STRESS, COBA and the NAG library are examples of this approach. The difference in principle is that in this case problems are identified and accommodated. In a 'ground-up' solution problems are eliminated.

Third, 'accommodating hosts'. In this case an environment is provided whereby an existing program written to use some operating system or other can run unaltered. Examples of this approach are TSX, RSTS/E and MUSIC-11 which run standard RT-11 programs and other systems which support CP/M as well as their native facilities. These systems are intended not only to run existing programs but also to provide additional facilities; for example time sharing by TSX etc. This approach may be implemented largely in hardware or entirely in software. As well as systems which seek to provide support of both old and new facilities there are 'clone' operating systems which seek to act exactly the same as each other.

There are of course solutions to portability which do not fall neatly into one class or another but contain elements of each. A solution which involves writing applications in a 'special language' which itself has implementations on various machines would fall halfway between the first two – the GENESYS system is such an example.

One crucial element of current programming technique which must be stressed is the use of software tools. During the program design phase the tools to be used must be carefully planned. The economic balance between programmer time and computer time has tipped strongly in favour of getting the computer to do as much of the work as possible. 'Desk-checking' and 'hand-debugging' techniques are no longer appropriate. Computers are much better at, for example, making systematic textual changes to a program body than people – when the programmer has decided what has to be done! Designers must acquaint themselves with whatever tools are available and if needs be design and construct their own.

The problems encountered in the ground-up approach have received much attention and it is obviously an intellectually stimulating exercise, but to what extent is it commercially justified? Certainly the early examples of portability tend to fall into the symbiotic category. The ground-up approach is gaining in popularity for two reasons. First, computers are now sufficiently cheap that systems can be installed to handle particular requirements so that their programs no longer have to co-exist with others on a single mainframe; and second, other applications suppliers are working to the same standards. Hence UNIX and MS/DOS in particular are gaining acceptance.

What techniques are available? An extremely important technique is the so-called 'bootstrapping' technique used for compiler implementation. This is of particular use in 'ground-up' systems where the target machine may have little or no existing software or where the existing software is incompatible with the target software system. Most of the software to be transported will be written in an appropriate high-level language and so once that language can be compiled on the new machine, much of the work will have been done.

Let us suppose the compiler is written in a language, quite possibly itself, capable of being compiled on machine A (the host machine) to produce machine code for machine A.

The code generation section of the compiler is then rewritten to produce the code of machine B (the target machine). This modified compiler is compiled by the 'old' compiler to produce a compiler on machine A which produces code for machine B. This new compiler is then used to compile the machine B compiler – typically itself. Thus a compiler to produce machine B code, running on machine B, is available.

Very simply that is the idea. Now, at least in theory, all the code that ran on machine A and written in the relevant language can now be recompiled and run on machine B.

One problem that remains of course is compilers other than that for the transported system language. A technique which has been applied is to ensure that all the compilers for the different languages produce not machine code but a 'pseudo-code' defined to be the target of all compilers. In this case the code generator which had to be redesigned at the start of this exercise will produce machine B code from the output of the other transported compilers. Another twist is to produce a machine B interpreter for the pseudo-code. Each new machine then 'merely' requires a new interpreter (and a bit of I/O code) and then even 'compiled' code can be executed. This latter approach must bear the overheads of interpretation.

The use of a well specified pseudo-code is a good example of the advantages of designing a system in layers with well defined interfaces. Very briefly that is the principle of bootstrapping.

The ground-up approach allows the designers to eliminate problems by removing options. Thus the designer can decide to use the ASCII character set and decide what convention to adopt throughout for the high-order bit. System-wide conventions can be established for the detection and treatment of arithmetic errors in a machine independent manner.

Nevertheless problems of arithmetic accuracy and program size remain, unless restrictive conventions are placed on these. It must be noted that applications portability depends on the effectiveness of the transfer of the system to the new machine and that in general the applications software will be portable only in that particular environment.

Symbiotic portability on the other hand requires the programmer of the application to address himself to the problems outlined in the earlier chapters. It is extremely unlikely that the program will work on a new host unchanged – so unlikely that success cannot be assured and transfer to each new machine will involve some effort if only to check that the program does work. The program design must take into account five main areas of incompatibility.

1 Choice of implementation language
2 Arithmetic facilities
3 Character representation
4 Program and data space
5 Input/output facilities.

Choice of implementation language

The designer must decide whether there is a widely available language adequate for his needs or whether he is going to implement his own. In general it makes better economic sense to plump for an existing language – traditionally this has been FORTRAN – despite its many deficiencies and most experience has been gained in its use as it is very widely available. Increasingly BASIC, Pascal and C are being used. Though there are standards for these languages, most compilers implement non-standard features. Obviously these must be avoided. The problem remains that standard features of the language may be imlemented in a non-standard way. To take a trivial but irritating example, if on input in FORTRAN a number is defined as I4 and written thus:

1bbb

(where b is a blank character)
FORTRAN specifies that it has the value 1000, i.e. trailing blanks are treated as numerically significant zeros. However, compilers exist which translate that input as 1. This latter approach seems more sensible, but it is incompatible with the specification. Only experience of each compiler will allow all such idiosyncrasies to be known.

Arithmetic facilities

In general integer arithmetic is used when calculating values used in the algorithm, for controlling iterations and for indexing data in arrays. The main problems arise in arithmetic accuracy for real number calculations.

Numerical analytic techniques are a highly specialized subject outside the scope of this discussion. Anyone designing portable software to cope with this class of problem would be well advised to refer to specialist papers. In somewhat simpler applications of real numbers the designer should consider the minimum acceptable degree of precision and ensure that changing from single to double precision, if a particular implementation of single precision is inadequate, can be done with simple textual changes to the source text. In FORTRAN this will require the program to contain declarations of all variables and not rely on implicit typing and use to define the variables. If at all possible it would be best to assume that integers can only assume values in the range ±32 767. If large integers are required for calculations a language which allows the declaration of higher-precision integers is desirable. It should be noted that the size of integer supported has implications for the size of arrays.

Languages which allow the manipulation of data pointers which are machine addresses but are represented and manipulated as integers are becoming more widely available. Pointers should be used with care and implicit assumptions about their size avoided. C has an interesting facility to declare long integers, short integers and integers, the latter being large enough to contain a pointer to any addressable element, but whose size is implementation-dependent.

To avoid overflow, underflow and loss of precision in both reals and integers the programmer should order his expressions with care using redundant parentheses, hoping that these will inhibit undesired and undesirable optimizations by the compiler.

Character representation

This seems a problem which should never have arisen. Nevertheless, it is a main area of complication. Some languages do not have explicit facilities for the handling of characters and strings at all. Often, especially in word machines, characters are stored in the left, or high order, bits of word. This will tend to ensure that, treated as integers, characters will appear to be numbers with large magnitudes, both positive and negative. Often comparisons are achieved by a load, subtract, test against zero sequence. This can lead to overflow, the effects of which, aside from producing the wrong answer, can either be ignored, cause a program exception or indeed produce an operating system exception which causes a program abort. Character comparisons, either of strings or single characters, unless the language provides explicitly for suitable and safe character handling, should be performed by functions, procedures or subroutines which return a value which represents the result.

Another problem, especially with FORTRAN, is that, if characters are stored in a 'real' number, assignment to another variable may invoke 'normalization' and thus destroy the character representation while retaining its irrelevant numeric value! It is often desirable to pack and unpack characters into computer words for the purpose of saving space both in memory and on backing store. This again should not be attempted using 'in-line' coding as sign extension and overflow problems may prevent a satisfactory solution using arithmetic operations but should be achieved via subroutine or function calls.

ASCII representation has certain regularities which are convenient, but these conveniences should be ignored. In particular the numbers 0–9 occupy consecutive integers. The upper case letters do the same and 1 bit distinguishes them from their lower case equivalents. It cannot be assumed that in all systems equivalent regularities occur. Collating sequences also vary between representations. The apparently time-consuming technique of translating characters on input into a consistent internal representation and translating them back again just before output may well be the best solution.

Program and data space

Programs expand to fill the available space. This does not refer to the use of complex dynamic storage allocation mechanisms but the fact that programmers only become interested in the size of their programs when they reach whatever limits are set by the hardware or the software. For portable software the problem of space manifests itself whether there is too much or too little.

There is usually a potential trade-off between program speed and size and between data requirements and program complexity. Accordingly the designer has to make a decision about his own priorities.

However, it is important to consider the acceptability of performance, for while it may be a major achievement to get a complex program performed on a very small machine, that same program may be judged inadequate on a large host. For any program there will be a minimum amount of storage which it needs to handle reasonably sized problems adequately. Below that size there will come a time when program overlays will be required.

The overlaying mechanisms will vary from host to host, nevertheless the possible need for overlaying should be taken into account throughout the design. Large-scale performance differences can follow from different overlay strategies used to implement the same algorithm on the same hardware. Being forced totally to restructure the program when the need for overlaying becomes apparent will not in general give the best results.

At the other end of the scale it is desirable to be able to use more memory if more than the minimum is available. Apart from obvious factors like not using constants embedded throughout a program to refer to what will be variable array sizes, what can be done?

The simplest approach (in languages which do not permit run-time array size definitions) is to ensure that various sizes of program can be readily produced by a systematic replacement of a few array bounds size definitions and the setting of the variables that refer to them.

The next approach is to implement a dynamic storage allocation mechanism which uses the memory available as efficiently as possible and provides mechanisms for handling data overflow.

A third approach adopted by the STRESS system is that the algorithms are designed to work on the minimum data representation. As new data are required, calls are made on a special routine. It is this routine that has the responsibility for using the memory and backing store to best advantage for a particular configuration though its storage is not dynamic. This mechanism also allows the designer to find the best trade-off between allowing a paged large address system to support huge arrays thus keeping all data in 'memory', and letting the program control its own input/output.

Input/output facilities

These probably represent the area of greatest differences between systems. As outlined in Chapter 3, it is an area in which not only the facilities offered by each system are different in capability but where access to essentially similar facilities is achieved by slightly or sometimes very different mechanisms. Unless the application can operate with a single input stream and produce a single output stream, it is probably best to define rigorously the input/ output requirements of the application, specify clearly the well defined methods to be used and invoke those facilities. Then for each new target system it will be necessary to implement the requirements in terms of the available mechanisms. It is desirable to make the demands on the host system as few and simple as possible since some of the more complex options may not be possible or can be achieved only with considerable difficulty. It must be a design aim to ensure the non-portable elements of a system are as few, simple and easy to implement as possible and expect only minimal features to be provided by the host.

Verification

Once all the design and programming is completed, there remains one task vital to having confidence that portability has been achieved, and that is verification of the product.

Comprehensive program testing is notoriously difficult, and complete and exhaustive testing probably impossible. The program should work correctly with correct data and reject all detectable errors. A programmer is likely, albeit subconsciously, to design tests to prove that a program works, rather than find out where it doesn't. It is desirable that the testing lies in other hands than the implementor's. It is important to build up as much test data and develop as many testing procedures as possible during the checking phase of the initial implementation so that new versions can be checked as automatically as possible. It is also important that if changes are made as a result of test failure, that all the tests are started from the beginning – it is not unknown for one bug to be fixed at the price of introducing another.

5

Ground-up systems

5

Ground-up systems

One extreme approach to portability is 'ground-up'. This is where a complete environment is transported from one computer to another. If this is done perfectly then all the architectural differences between the systems will be completely hidden. A user will not be able to detect any differences between the various implementations.

If the various machines have radically different facilities, e.g. if one has memory management and a very large address space and the other is restricted to a total of 64 KB, then a choice must be made between restricting each implementation to have only the facilities of the most restricted or accepting a degree of lack of compatibility. This again will depend on how general the systems facilities are. If the system provides compilers for a large number of languages generating in-line code then it is likely that these will give access to the actual hardware facilities and thus reduce applications portability. Complete portability can only be bought at the price of arbitrary restrictions.

The systems covered in this chapter are CP/M, UNIX, MS/DOS, and Micro COBOL and BOS. This list is not exhaustive but is representative of different techniques and is thus a reasonable cross-section. The choice is not meant to imply that there are no other systems with worthwhile and interesting features or that the other systems are in any way inferior.

CP/M

CP/M is a standard single-user operating system. It is widely used both in the home computer market and in business and scientific applications. Accordingly it is one of the most widely used operating systems. Hence there is a vast range of software written and available for CP/M systems. It is written for 8080 micros and runs on computers which interpret 8080 instructions which means the 8085 and Z80 CPUS, as well as 8080s. It is supplied and controlled by Digital Research. Three main components are supplied: the Console Command Processor (CCP), Basic Disk Operating System (BDOS) and Basic Input/Output System (BIOS).

The only modifications needed for CP/M are first, a mechanism to alter the amount of memory the system expects. A utility program is provided to achieve this. Second, allowance for different I/O drivers. As mentioned earlier, even with the same CPU, systems will differ in their I/O mechanisms. To allow for these differences it is necessary to modify the BIOS.

Differences in I/O driver hardware may give rise to format differences between floppy discs.

As a result of such a simple but well defined approach CP/M has become a very widely used vehicle for software portability.

It must, of course, be recognized that this portability is achieved over a well defined subset of computers only.

One development following from this limitation is a hardware-supported version for the Apple computer which itself uses the 6502 microprocessor. This hardware incorporates a Z80 computer. The success of this approach opens wide a fascinating range of possibilities for program portability.

CP/M is designed and implemented for one particular order-code (the Intel 8080) which happens, for whatever reason, to be the processor in a very wide range of microcomputer products from a wide range of suppliers.

The portability of UNIX

UNIX is an operating system written at Bell Laboratories. It is a multi-user system supporting a complex filing system and providing elegant mechanisms for communications between symbiotic tasks. Until 1982 it was available only for educational purposes or at a very high price with very little support directly from Western Electric. This has changed and the system is widely available on many different computers.

It was originally written in Assembler to run on an old DEC computer. In due course it was re-written in C to run on PDP/11s with memory management. This latter requirement is important as the facilities provided by the PDP memory management and user/kernel modes provide the necessary protection required to implement a secure multi-programming system.

The C language was designed as a suitable language in which it was possible to write all the components of an operating system right down to the level of device drivers on the PDP/11. It has an innovative approach to integer representation, which if used rigorously, minimizes problems of portability.

There is a detailed paper describing the problems encountered in moving this C-based system to an Interdata computer (Johnson and Ritchie, 1978). As explained in the paper this became an iterative process involving modifications both to the UNIX code and the C language and compiler.

The Computing Science Research Centre at Bell Laboratories had a history of interest in program portability and after the design of C on PDP/11 produced C compilers for the Honeywell 6000 and IBM 370 mainframes. This process, while largely successful, revealed problems in two areas. The first was the maintenance of compatability between the various compilers as each was implemented independently and the C language itself was not stable but was being developed in the light of experience.

The second was that program portability was adversely affected more by the underlying host operating systems than by the differences in C or by the underlying machine architecture. This problem showed itself both because the applications programs being transported used UNIX conventions and because some UNIX facilities proved impossible to implement in terms of the host operating system. It also transpired that restrictions in the host system utilities (loader's librarians, etc.) which were being used made changes necessary in C. Nevertheless it proved possible to move large applications programs reasonably easily between systems.

However, the problems encountered were sufficiently great to suggest the desirability of transporting not only the applications code, but also the operating system itself.

This decision must be seen in the context of its period in the early 1970s. In the light of the advances in computing made in the last 15 years, it may be difficult to realize that the idea of an independent operating system for productive use was unusual then. It was not unique. University departments of computing science were designing and implementing operating systems but they were more concerned with advancing concepts and implementing facilities than with producing systems for everyday production computing. Computers were still relatively expensive and therefore computer time was a scarce resource and 'minis' were still used on a small scale for relatively small-scale problems. It was an implicit assumption that users would use the manufacturer's operating system (or indeed systems) for this was the period when many manufacturers took decisions which resulted in their providing a variety of operating systems on the same architecture! The concept of machine ranges, where manufacturers standardized on a common order code for their variously priced offerings, has not led to a standard operating system across these same ranges – let alone a standard across different ranges.

Some research had been undertaken into transportable operating systems but UNIX was by then in wide use. The project had to proceed on the assumption that the system to be transported already existed. The implementation strategy has three elements.

1   A C compiler readily adaptable to produce code for a variety of machines.
2   Extensions of C to ease the portability of C programs and to aid mechanical recognition of non-portable constructions.
3   The production of UNIX in this portable C with the identification and isolation of non-portable machine-specific areas.

The chosen host was an Inderdata 8/32 computer. This was markedly different from the PDP/11 architecture and it is interesting to note that amongst the reasons for choosing it was the fact that it had a large address space and thus could run programs that could not be handled on the PDP/11. In other words this project essentially contained elements of non-portability!

The first goal to be achieved was the portable C compiler. This was a new compiler designed to be readily modified to produce code for a variety of machines. It turned out that approximately 80 per cent of the code was the same in all versions. It also had the advantage that most maintenance changes can be readily applied to all implementations.

The process of moving UNIX itself was divisible into the various elements which comprise the operating system. Some of these are inherently machine-dependent and others theoretically machine-independent.

The essentially machine-specific elements of UNIX fall into two major categories. The first comprises the basic hardware interface routines which handle, as a set of primitives, machine idiosyncrasies such as basic I/O operations, machine state changes for memory management and task switching, moving data between address spaces (e.g. user to system). Other routines are required for handling interrupts (i.e. external event signals) and traps (system calls, machine exceptions) and interfacing these in a C compatible way with the rest of the operating system. These are written in Assembler.

The next machine-dependent part is that concerned with device drivers. These are written in C but must cope with the differences between the implementations of different physical devices. The interface between these routines and the rest of UNIX remained intact and the PDP/11 versions provided a code model for the structure and apparently much of the code for the Interdata version.

The third element was the largest and proved very largely portable. The success was achieved by identifying what were essentially errors of coding style in the original version. This involved changing literal constants to compile-time parameters and ensuring correct typing of all variables. Some differences were pathological and were concerned with direction of stack growth, memory management differences and processor trap handling.

Problems were encountered and overcome during the initial bootstrapping concerned with the order of byte storage in words and with floating point representation.

The above describes briefly some of the problems encountered and overcome in transporting UNIX to the Interdata 8/32.

The actual route followed for this transfer was to get the C compiler running independently on the Interdata machine in a simple 'stand alone' mode. This was then used to compile as many C programs as could be found with limited I/O requirements and these were used to debug the compiler. Once this was working UNIX was transferred piecemeal until the entire system was transported.

At about the same time another route was employed in Australia to transport UNIX to Interdata 7/32. In this case the C compiler was adapted from the PDP/11 to produce Interdata code running under the Interdata operating system and then the UNIX system was built up as a task under the Interdata system, until enough of it was working so that it could work independently.

The above describes the transfer of UNIX from its original PDP/11 host to two Interdata machines.

Since that work was done the popularity of UNIX has grown. There are many reasons for this. First, UNIX is a good operating system – that makes it unusual but not unique. Second, it has available with it a great range of utility software. Third, it was implemented initially on one of the most widely available 16-bit minis. Fourth, it was made available to educational establishments at an attractive price. Thus it has been exposed widely to many students, many of whom are now actively employed in the outside world of computing. This fact, plus a change in the legal position in the USA, has led to a multiplicity of UNIX systems on a wide range of hardware.

There are three main sources of UNIX systems (all of which appear under different trade names). The first is from Bell Laboratories themselves, who, for a fee, make available a source version of UNIX in C plus a portable C compiler. The second is direct from Bell Laboratories, as a running system. The third is from independent implementors of UNIX look-alikes, who have, entirely properly, implemented systems which support UNIX systems calls and subroutine libraries. Further to complicate the issue there are several versions of official UNIX available which differ in detail and in some important detail at that. These include 'Version 7' and 'System III'. Moves are currently afoot to define an acceptable general specification. The large installed base and the multiplicity of suppliers of UNIX systems make this an uphill struggle.

In addition to the opportunities for confusion afforded by the various origins, there is the further position of implementation differences between the microprocessors for which UNIX is available. The I/O systems and memory management strategies implemented on various Z8000 and 68000 processors will vary.

The 'standard' UNIX versions are all derived from the C version for PDP/11 and the portable compiler. The task of the implementor of UNIX on new hardware is thus simpler than the original transportation described above. However, in the Johnson and Ritchie paper describing the problems of code generation is the telling and perhaps prophetic sentence: 'The calling sequence [i.e. for subroutines and system entry] is very important to the efficiency of the result and takes considerable knowledge and imagination to design properly'. It is the case that there are non-PDP/11 versions of UNIX but on the same CPU between which there are code generation and calling sequence incompatibilities, so that there is no compatibility of compiled code.

Differences therefore will become apparent in the details of facilities implemented and in the generated code itself.

The commercial UNIX User Group (/USR/GROUP) is producing an external specification standard of system and subroutine calls in an effort to produce an agreed implementation standard. As each of the independently named 'UNIX' systems is the product of a single software house, though marketed through agents, it is likely that their particular products will be consistent and compatible with each other.

However, independent suppliers of software for UNIX systems will have to be aware of and take steps to overcome the inconsistencies.

Throughout this discussion of UNIX runs a discussion of C. UNIX relies heavily on C not only as systems language but also as applications language. The problem still remains of other languages. These will have to be produced and transported to new architectures. It must be realized that each system will need compilers that generate code appropriate not only to the particular order code but to the conventions of a particular implementation.

With the more general availability of UNIX outside the educational environment has come a degree of criticism leading to a variety of proposals for improvements. It follows that as the system is now in the hands of various implementors, there is a strong possibility that systems will diverge from the original *de facto* standard.

One interesting footnote to UNIX is one success of the Onyx system. Onyx is a UNIX implementation on the Zilog Z8000. COBOL programs have been successfully transported from the Texas Instruments 990/DX10 system to the Z80 and then to the Z8000. This process has been achieved by transporting a portable COBOL compiler from the Texas to Onyx. The only big problems encountered on the way have been a need to overlay on the Z80 and the need to change file headers under Onyx.

MS/DOS

MS/DOS is another ground-up system that has achieved enormous success. It is also well known as PC/DOS. This is a proprietary system produced by Microsoft for the Intel 8086 and compatible processors. Because of the great success of the IBM PC, the PC architecture became a *de facto* standard, as did its operating system. In this case each host configuration contains a ROM BIOS – Basic Input Output System. This program must support a well defined set of functions in a well defined manner.

Thus this system is available only on systems which comply with certain core requirements. The problem for the transportation of applications programs between MS/DOS systems is that many such programs use facilities not defined in that common core, and therefore differ from implementation to implementation.

Micro COBOL

Micro COBOL is one example of the embedded approach which has been conspicuously successful as an example of portable software. It is a proprietary product supplied and maintained by a single company (MPSL).

The Micro COBOL/BOS system has developed over more than 12 years from the original intention to run one applications program on two micros. Applications portability was its design aim. The achievement of this goal lead to the definition of Micro COBOL – a COBOL-like language with extensions, and BOS, an operating system which could be transported to new hardware.

The total product is defined by MPSL to the extent that it supplies the compiler, utilities, operating system and device drivers. It has been successfully implemented on over 50 computer types. It is interesting to note that it has been found necessary to divide target machines both by architecture and by individual implementations of the hardware.

An architecture in this context is an order code or instruction set. Architectures supported include Intel 8080, 8085, Zilog, 8056; Motorola 6800, 6809, 68000; Data General Nova; DEC PDP; Texas Instruments TIl 9900 and IBM Series 1.

Some of these CPUs are however available in different implementations so that I/O is provided differently between systems with the same CPU.

How then has this success been achieved? Micro COBOL is implemented interpretively and is itself used as the system's implementation language. The compiler translates the source code into a well defined intermediate code. It follows then that significant amounts of program can be transferred to a new system in compiled format.

What is required is that for each new architecture a new interpreter should be written. For reasons of efficiency, certain routines are written in Assembler. The code that needs to be written for each processor type is the interpreter and the 'executives'. Each different processor implementation requires a set of device drivers.

Micro COBOL the language has been defined not only to be used for the applications programs but also has facilities allowing it to be used to write the BOS monitor programs. One consequence of this approach is that when a new set of machine code routines has been written, if the monitor system works, then it is extremely likely that all the applications programs will also work.

The success of this approach to portability is based not only on the conceptual framework but also on a rigorous and complete definition of the interfaces and specifications. The interpreter implements a pseudo-machine and this pseudo-machine code is the target code of the compiler. It can also be used as a programming language itself. The design of the pseudo-machine is of great importance in the effectiveness of the final product. It is necessary that it should meet several criteria. First, it should allow code to be compiled into reasonable compact representation, as naturally as possible. Second, it must be complete and rigorous. All actions and particularly exception actions must be defined. Third, it must be possible to write efficient interpreters on even the simplest of micros, compactly.

One interesting facility designed into this pseudo-code is the ability to escape into machine code. As this is always necessary, if undesirable, it is much better to accept the need and provide the necessary interfaces, than to be *ad hoc*.

The next carefully defined topic is input/output. This is explicitly separated into basic I/O – for example read a sector on disc, write a character to a terminal – and the I/O services provided – open a file, input a character string. This separation allows decoupling between the code needed to handle a particular device and the operations available to an applications code. The protocols available for each device type are called in this system 'executives'.

It is instructive to compare the Micro-COBOL route with the UNIX route. In both cases the basic I/O and machine interface (the primitives) have to be rewritten in Assembler. Micro-COBOL executives are conceptually similar to UNIX device handlers. In the case of Micro-COBOL, this code is always rewritten in Assembler for reasons solely of efficiency. In UNIX – as C compiles into machine code, they are written in C, but require modification for each architecture. The BOS system is then invariant across systems while the UNIX kernel requires minor modifications to handle architectural differences.

The systems discussed above are representative of various approaches to program design, implementation and distribution. All four are proprietary products but each is distributed differently. CP/M is tightly controlled by Digital Research who produce themselves copies of the standard system. A degree of tailoring to particular configurations can then be performed by end users or by distributors. BOS is produced by MPSL for each target configuration and is distributed by themselves or agents as final versions. UNIX is licensed to anyone paying the licence fee and they then perform the necessary transportations. It is now available from both software houses and manufacturers who supply versions for their particular machines. MS/DOS is sold with the various PC clones, each manufacturer's version may have minor cosmetic changes.

Can any general conclusions be drawn from examining these four ground-up systems? Perhaps the most noticeable common feature is that each defines its own standards. They make no concessions to the past and do not try to use existing programs or conventions. The price the user must pay for their advantages is to accept the new way of doing things.

Each has achieved its portability by rigorously separating machine-dependent elements from the machine specifics and thus allowing for unforeseen problems to be isolated before they occur and so solved as they occur.

None of the systems is transparent to user addressability. This implies that though program portability between implementations is achievable, there remains the problem of program size. This must still be solved by the programmer.

6
Emulation

6

Emulation

This is a mechanism to achieve portability of existing programs which were not originally implemented to be portable. It is achieved by providing a new environment in which they may execute which appears identical to the program, where an environment includes some sort of order-code processor and at least the operating system input/output functions.

There are two main reasons for following this course of action and several mechanisms available for achieving it. The first reason is to allow existing programs to run on a new machine or operating system. Historically certain systems have attracted a considerable degree of success so that there are many useful programs available under it. Again a manufacturer may produce a new system and his customers will want to continue running their existing programs. No longer do manufacturers blithely expect their customers to rewrite all their programs when they buy a new machine. Indeed manufacturers may well want to be able to run programs currently available on other manufacturers' machines which provide different

71

environments. How then can this be achieved. There are two main mechanisms available – hardware and software.

Hardware mechanisms

Technological change has lead to the position where the order code of any given computer is often implemented not, as is traditional, with hard-wired logic, but via micro-code. This is in itself a form of emulation. The 'basic' order code of the computer is not that 'seen' by the compilers and Assembler but is one both simpler and much faster in which a micro-code program is written to implement the defined user order code.

This order-code processor can itself be implemented using 'bit-sliced' 'microprocessors' or by an individually designed 'microprocessor'. Note that this is a different use of the word 'microprocessor' from that used to describe VLSI single chip CPUs – though of course these can themselves be implemented via micro-coding techniques. The main disadvantage of this approach to computer design is that it is inherently slower than the best achievable performance using 'hard-wired' techniques. This disadvantage is irrelevant except in the very highest performance mainframes as the microprocessor is very much faster than the economically available main-memories. A facility provided by the use of such microprocessing techniques is the ability to implement more than one order code 'simultaneously' in the same computer. Sometimes micro-coded central processors are completely 'soft', that is, the control store (the internal memory which contains the program to implement the order code) can itself be written to. Thus a new micro-program emulating a different order code can be installed easily (this does not imply that it can be written easily). If there is a facility to have more than one micro-program and to switch between them then the appropriate order code can be chosen 'on the fly'. It is more usual for the micro-program to be contained in read only memories (ROM) which reduces flexibility but provides security from interference caused by inadvertent changes to the micro-code and ensures that the computer will be able to run when powered up!

Depending on the available size of the control store and the size of the emulating programs, it is possible to include programs to emulate more than one order code. Mechanisms are then provided to switch 'modes' in the host computer and thus execute a different order code. Some manufacturers use this sort of mechanism to support not only their current order code but also to allow the execution of programs written in a previous code. Of course such compatability can be provided in totally hard-wired logic, but the trend is towards micro coded emulations.

Even when the order code can be directly executed there remains the problem of operating system incompatabilities. Despite the fact that the old order code can still be executed, the operating system will be written in the new order code and inevitably will contain new facilities. Even if it supports all the facilities of the old operating system as subset, it is unlikely that these are referenced and accessed identically. Thus it is necessary for the manufacturer seeking to provide portability not only to implement two (or more) order codes on a single CPU but to provide links in the new operating system to support the features of the old. This again emphasizes the importance of the operating system environment in the achievement of portability.

There is another hardware path to emulation. This is done not by emulating previous hardware, but by including it in another configuration. One example is the Z80 card available for the Apple II – a 6502 system. As a result of careful design of the original Apple and some ingenious programming the Apple becomes a CP/M system and the Z80 uses the memory and I/O facilities of the original machine. There are other machines available in which CP/M support is achieved by including a 8080 or Z80 processor which the main processor can direct to execute a particular program. This approach is made economically feasible because a CPU now costs about the same as a floppy disc, so even if the software to emulate the processor were free it would cost as much to distribute the program as the processor it emulates would cost to buy. Moreover there can be no misunderstandings of the sort that can be made by an emulation program of exactly how the processor functions and there is no speed disadvantage!

Software mechanisms

The problems in providing operating system emulators are very similar. In this approach the designer of a new operating system includes, as a subset, all the facilities of the other. The reason for doing this is either because the new system offers additional facilities or because the new system is an implementation by different code of the old. An example of the first approach is RT-11 emulation. RT-11 is a DEC operating system designed for smaller PDP/11s. It is extremely popular and there is good software available for it from many sources. Thus there is a strong motivation to incorporate its facilities into other more sophisticated PDP/11 operating systems. Because the programs are, more often than not, available only in loadable binary image form, it only makes sense to emulate RT-11 on PDP/11s.

How is this achieved? The problems lie in two areas. First, as the new system is likely to be more powerful, its additional facilities may make the implementation of the old facilities, as some of these will be cruder than their more modern equivalents, more difficult. Second, as the new system will tend strongly, for legal as well as technical reasons, to be completely new code, there will be differences in implementation.

How then is this sort of emulation achieved? One way is the 'run-time system' approach. RT-11 programs expect to share their memory with a monitor program which is the operating system. Thus it is possible to replace the original monitor with a program whose function is not to implement the RT-11 functions itself but to map them into logically equivalent functions supported by the new system and then to call the host operating system to perform the tasks it understands. To do this it is necessary to alert the host not to declare RT-11 system calls illegal but instead to pass them to some 'run-time' system. The run-time system then interprets the old system call and constructs the appropriate call on the new facilities to make the new operating system perform the desired actions. Any returned information must be transformed into the format expected by the old application before it is passed back.

Another way is for the new system to contain the system calls of the old system as a subset of the new. The mechanism for calling new system facilities must then be designed to take into account the original calling sequences and provide support for them.

One route adopted is to notice that the format used by RT-11 calls is capable of extension. The PDP/11 order code includes several 'trap instructions'. One of these, the so-called emulator trap (EMT), contains an 8-bit code. RT-11 uses the codes 374 and 375 (octal) to specify groups of system functions. The associated parameter list contains a further code to identify which function in the group is required. Not all values of this sub-code are meaningful in RT-11, so it is possible to define extra functions by defining additional codes. One obvious risk is that RT-11 itself is not static and its implementors might choose to use one of the same sub-codes in some later release.

Another approach adopted by MUSIC-11 is to note there are several EMT codes that are never used. One of these (EMT 373) was chosen and the word following the instruction was used to contain the defining code for the appropriate function in MUSIC. This method runs the risk that the chosen gap be filled at some later stage. It does have two compensating advantages. First, the two calling mechanisms are totally disjoint, which allows MUSIC to have its own completely separate set of system functions. There are for example two possible calls to print a character string, though of course they use the same code almost entirely. The second advantage is that the MUSIC calling sequence is defined to be the same as the major applications language used so that source programs can call system functions directly via a very simple interface module.

There are two practical problems for the implementor of emulation programs. One is that the system being emulated will inevitably be incompletely documented. There will be some side-effects, not predictable from the documentation, which will have been used by some programmers because they have proved useful. This is the case with both operating systems and central processors. The other problem can occur when multiple error conditions arise simultaneously. Suppose the program attempts to open a file for reading which is not in the directory, on a unit which is already associated with another file. This contains two errors and the order in which the two systems perform their error checks may differ. This would cause execution to follow different paths through the emulated program than would have been the case in the original environment, and thus it would produce results which are not the same as when the program was in its original environment.

If the program to be emulated is in source form, then it is possible to construct a 'bounce' library package. This approach is similar to the 'run-time' system approach but assumes that the source program calls can be made directly to a library of 'bounce' routines and that these links are made at load time. In these circumstances there is no requirement for the operating system to provide an escape mechanism back to the user to handle 'error' conditions. It is a reasonable approach to the design of portable programs to define a set of pseudo-operating system facilities which are then implemented afresh on each host. In this case the facilities to be supported are those defined by another operating system and so not under the control of the implementor. To achieve success with this route it may be necessary to know in some considerable detail the code generated by the compiler to invoke those facilities. A mechanism often employed is the definition of names of system library routines using characters rejected by the compilers, i.e. to include $ (dollar signs) or . (period or full stop). A certain amount of ingenuity is sometimes required both to find out what needs to be done and then to do it.

Increasingly operating systems and computers are becoming less autocratic, which is of considerable assistance to the writers of emulators. Instead of collapsing completely when faced with an exceptional condition (e.g. an unimplemented instruction or an unsupported supervisor call) the user is offered the opportunity to specify mechanisms which are invoked by the operating system and which allow him to try to cope himself.

A more traditional form of emulation is order code emulation. A program is written which interprets the order of another computer (or even itself). This approach has some advantages which still remain despite the economic changes mentioned above. The problem always remains, as with all emulations, that the host system is not identical to the original. However it is a useful approach to adopt in two areas.

The first is the traditional area of running 'old' programs on a new machine. The desirability of this is self-evident and the cost of producing the emulator and the inherent loss of execution speed may well be a price worth paying. The second area is of growing importance. As prices drop computers are being used in cars, washing machines, toys etc. Patently these will not contain full systems with terminals, screens and other peripherals. The programs incorporated in these devices will have to be written and tested on other systems. By using the full panoply of editors, filing systems and compilers, the production of these programs can be simplified. Their testing can be made easier by building emulators which contain facilities not provided by the target hardware system. For example, and this is one reason for emulating the host processor itself, there may be no instruction-tracing or single-stepping option on the target machine.

The construction of an emulator with trace, break point and illegal instruction-trapping options may pay considerable dividends when developing programs, which might well contain some assembly code elements, which are going to be supplied in huge quantities. Program maintenance in this sort of application is not as simple as sending out a new version on magnetic tape to a small handful of technically competent users. There is an economic requirement to make such systems with the minimum number of hardware components and this may lead to requiring that programs are kept to a small size. This requirement might imply more machine code as a proportion of the total than would be strictly necessary and a proper support system, which allows machine code to be transported easily from the test environment to the working environment, will pay dividends.

Order code emulators are available for several of the more popular instruction sets. They are just interpreters, as are BASIC interpreters. The interpreter seeks to copy the actions of the target machine. One mechanism is to use the order code to decide which of a set of subroutines to call. Apart from the problem of knowing exactly what the original hardware will do under certain unusual conditions, there is the problem of size for, in general, the emulator occupies part of the same logical space as the emulated code. This may restrict the size of program that can be emulated. Detecting carry and overflow on 8-bit operands will require additional programming on 16-bit and larger word size machines. It can be seen that such emulators will require many more instructions to be executed than the original code needed to produce the same result. There is an inevitable loss of efficiency.

In this chapter we have seen that it is possible to use a variety of techniques to provide new environments which protect an investment in software made in the past. With the possible exception of the 'bounce package' technique, the methods are rather complex technically and rather expensive to implement.

7

Symbiotic systems

SYMBIOTIC SYSTEMS

7

Symbiotic systems

STRESS-II

Symbiotic systems are those designed to run on a large range of host machines, using only the tools regularly available on those systems. In this chapter we consider a variety of successful programs adopting this philosophy.

STRESS is a program for analysing skeletal structures. The program described is STRESS-II. It is a product of Euro Computer Systems Ltd. The original version of STRESS was written to be portable and was successfully implemented on 21 different systems. While this proved successful, moving the program to a new system required a lot of skill. STRESS-II is a reorganized program to simplify the transfers to new installations. The opportunity was taken to improve certain aspects of the program and to remove certain constraints.

STRESS-II achieves its success in two ways. The first is by algorithmic design techniques which allow the size of problem that can be tackled to be decoupled from the size of machine available and by imposing conventions on the representation of character data. The other is by rigorously separating all the necessarily machine-specific elements of the program into a single subroutine which then needs implementing anew on each target system. The distribution kit comprises the machine independent program, the machine dependent subroutine and the documentation.

The machine-independent code body requires only one change. The code needs to know how many integers there are in one real. Standard FORTRAN states that this shall be one, although it is usually one for 'large machines' and two for minis and micros. It can however be three. This is the only change needed – or indeed permitted.

For small machines overlaying may be required, the required overlay structure is clearly defined in the documentation. For this approach to be effective, the overlaying system of the host must not require textual changes to the program.

The machine-independent part is written in a version of FORTRAN consistent with both ANSI FORTRAN and ANSI FORTRAN 77 and comprises some 2800 statements.

The machine-dependent section comprises about 600 FORTRAN statements, two-thirds of which are comments. The executable statements are provided for one particular system, and are a model of the code to be implemented for each new and different target system.

This section comprises one subroutine CHAN and several subroutines called by CHAN. CHAN has an implementation-independent interface and is called from the machine-independent code. It is responsible for all input/output operations. It transmits records to and from the user terminal, opens and closes files, transmits records between the user program and scratch files and enforces the chosen character representation.

Characters are in fact stored as ASCII with the parity bit set, stored in the low-order bits of integer variables. There is therefore no problem with packing or unpacking or with the sign bit. All character manipulations other than those enforcing this coding are performed in the machine independent coding.

CHAN expects to be able to use as many as 13 files on 13 channels. It expects to be able to handle seven unformatted scratch files. It checks the legality of operation against each channel as not all channels have the same characteristics.

The problem of machine size is the responsibility of a subroutine DISKIO. This subroutine transmits records to or from a direct-access file. Not only does it perform the I/O, making the necessary input/output calls, but it also manages a disc cache system designed to minimize physical I/O and maps the various record lengths on to 'pages'; the size of which is chosen to reflect the organization of the data on disc. While each channel has a fixed length, determined when the call to open the file is made, each channel may have a different length. This solves neatly the problems of the record size supported by the input/output system and uses the available memory as efficiently as possible to improve program performance.

Also provided is a set of test data. When it is believed that a successful transportation is complete, the user runs the program with these data. The results are sent back to the supplier who validates them.

COBA

COBA is a program for the economic evaluation of road improvement schemes. It was written for the Department of Transport by Wootton, Jeffreys and Partners.

It can be run using 17 different FORTRAN compilers. This does not mean 17 different computers. There are sufficient differences between IBM operating systems on the same computer for different code to be required for each system. The machines supported range from large CDC computers to CP/M micros.

There are two versions of the program: one handles 250 links and the other 50 links (links are the basic elements in the road network models). The CP/M version has been made smaller by removing error message text and outputting error numbers. It has also required that a large common array be implemented as a direct-access file. Some versions are overlayed, and indeed for the ICL 1900, there is a choice between a small memory version and a larger, faster version.

The program text is maintained as a single file and the various versions are produced using GENERATOR.

How was the portability achieved? First, the language used was an empirically selected FORTRAN sub-set, chosen to be available on all compilers. Features of FORTRAN about which there was any doubt were not used. Over time the *de facto* restrictions have been relaxed in the light of experience. For example, DATA statements are used only in code specific to a particular system; otherwise initialization is by assignment statements.

Second, arithmetic problems were considered in the program design and all input data were checked for range before any arithmetic operations were performed. All real arithmetic is single-precision, and rounding errors are known to be less than the inaccuracies in the input data.

Character comparisons are performed by Functions, and the main program is interested only in whether two characters are or are not the same so that collating sequence is irrelevant. Character assignments are also performed by a subroutine. These Functions and subroutines are implemented afresh for each new target system.

It has been found empirically to be the case that an intermediate binary file used by the program presents no problems provided that the corresponding READ and WRITE statements are identical, ensuring an exact match of records. All other I/O is simple sequential and has proved to be no problem. On most systems it proves possible to open the necessary files using the job control language, external to the program.

COBA is kept as a single source file for all versions. It contains special 'driver' format card images. These are used to direct GENERATOR which is a preprocessor. GENERATOR selectively produces a version appropriate to a particular target compiler. It does this by textual substitutions and by conditional selection of sections of code. The process is mechanical and is intended as an aid to program maintenance, ensuring that there is only one source file. However, that source file contains all the machine-specific code and this has to be hand coded for each target system.

TRAMP

This is another Wootton, Jeffreys and Partners program. It is a modelling program for road/traffic networks. The size of networks handled has not proved a problem over a large range of machines. This is a consequence not so much of algorithmic design but mostly because of the relatively small size of such networks in practice.

This program was written in FORTRAN IV adhering strictly to the standard and avoiding the logical IF statement. It was designed with 16 bit integers as the target accuracy. A consequence of this decision and also of the nature of the data to be represented led to the implementation of an internal numerical representation. Values are stored in a pseudo floating point form, though arithmetic operations are performed with the inbuilt arithmetic. The internal representation, which uses only 15 bits allows adequate accuracy for the data and can be manipulated by integer arithmetic, in FORTRAN, consistently on all target machines. It was also decided not to rely on the random number generator provided by the system as this would give rise to inconsistencies between implementations.

The original intention was that by choosing to code in a strict standard version of FORTRAN IV and by choosing to use 16-bit integers as a maximum, one version of source would be portable. This proved not to be the case. The problems arose in two areas. The first is fairly intractable and concerns FORTRAN input/output. If FORTRAN format statements are used to read input data and those data are incorrectly coded, e.g. an alphabetic character is punched in a numeric field, the error is deleted by the I/O package and the user can do little about it. Systems in general do not even make the identification of such erroneous data easy. This is important since a good program tries not only to produce correct results with correct data, but to help the user correct his input data when necessary. The answer is to read in all the data in character format, check them for correct numerical format and then translate numeric strings into internal format. Not all FORTRAN compilers have ENCODE and DECODE statements which perform this translation and though they are often available they are not implementd in a standard way. When absent, code has to be supplied to perform the translation.

The other remaining problem was character comparison. The program design kept this to the minimum. Embedded in the data deck are single characters to mark various data types. Even reading this single character as A1 (which is FORTRAN for 'put a single character into a single word') and performing an arithmetic IF, which involves a subtraction, was found to produce problems and so special coding had to be introduced.

The experience of TRAMP showed that even with the careful and deliberate design of programs to use only the highest common factor between machines, problems still remained that need machine-specific solutions.

8

Compiler portability

8
Compiler portability

This chapter discusses the problems, and some solutions, of transporting compilers. The aim of transporting compilers is to make a language available on a new computer. The terms 'host machine' and 'target machine' are used. The host machine is the computer on which the compiler runs. The target machine is the one on which the compiled program will run. The host and the target are usually the same for most commercially available compilers.

Why discuss this relatively arcane subject? First, the work done in this area is interesting for the consideration of portability as a whole. Second, there may be a case for producing a portable compiler as a tool in a large software project to ease applications portability.

Traditionally there have been two constraints on the use of high-level languages and these have influenced the design of compilers. These are speed of compilation and speed of execution of compiled code. Changing economic conditions have changed the emphasis. It may now well be that a relatively slow compilation process is acceptable if the results are particularly useful.

There has probably been more work done on compiler portability than on any other aspect of portability. Certainly many papers have been published. There are many reasons for this. The best theoretical reason is that if it can be achieved, then programs written in the language transported will themselves be portable. Another reason is that the work can be done on existing computers and used by others, something not true of operating systems development. In practice, of course, the underlying operating system and hardware tend to obtrude and thus prevent complete transparency.

What then are the aspects of a compiler that are relevant to portability? A compiler is a program that runs on a computer and translates one computer language to another. In that crude description there are three important elements. First, the compiler is itself a program; second, it recognizes the syntax of a language; and third, it produces as output another language. The second aspect of this process, language recognition, is well described in many papers and books on the design of compilers and is not of the essence in the portability of the compiler.

It is of course desirable that all compilers claiming to compile language 'X' should recognize the same definition of 'X'. In practice for the popular languages, there are many implementations of each language. These compilers are of different designs, and this may lead to the syntactic differences referred to earlier. However, for a consideration of compiler portability we can afford to ignore the recognition algorithms and aspects such as symbol table handling, it being reasonable to assume that these algorithms will be capable of implementation on all host machines.

The problems we are then left to resolve are the language in which the compiler is written; and the output language. The output language has two important aspects.

First, it must represent the semantic content of the recognized syntax – this has been referred to as the 'witchcraft' of compiler writing. This semantic representation is the process of 'code' generation. The generated code may be:

1 another high-level language (e.g. Pascal into C);
2 the assembly language of the target computers;
3 the loadable binary format of the target computer; or
4 the machine code of an abstract machine.

Each of these solutions has its advantages and problems. The first, producing another high-level language, is not widely used. It is just not possible to map between all language pairs acceptably, though some combinations may be possible.

The technique of producing the assembly language of the target machine has two practical advantages. One is that it is easier than producing loadable binary and the other is that it is readily readable by people, and thus simplifies the debugging process.

Loadable binary format, which is the customary output medium for compilers supplied by manufacturers, has the twin advantages of speed and compactness. It has the significant disadvantage of requiring an understanding of the binary formats used by a particular loader (linkage editor). These are highly idiosyncratic and frequently undocumented.

Finally there is the 'abstract machine' code concept. This has the considerable advantage that it can be independent of any particular target computer. However, to execute it, it requires either further translation into target machine code, or it needs an interpreter to be written to run on the target machine.

It can be seen that all these approaches, except the production of loadable binary, require further processing of the output before loading and execution. Another compilation or assembly phase will take more time before the final executable program is ready. This may be a price worth paying.

The problems of producing target code, whether as Assembler or binary require the design of the code generators for each target system. Techniques for simplifying this process have been developed but detailed work is nevertheless required to understand the target order code and to produce the mapping of the semantics on to this order code. Differences caused by such mappings can produce problems for portability of source code. This is because differences between the facilities provided by different order codes and in the code generation algorithms can give rise to incompatibilities between two similar compilers for the same language on different machines.

The concept of generating code for an abstract machine is an old one. There have been many attempts to define such machines over the years but none has been universally accepted. Frequently the abstract machine is tailored to express well the language being compiled. This then tends to diminish one of the main potential advantages of the technique as it may not be so suitable for the next language to be compiled. Suppose there could be defined an abstract machine which would readily support all known languages, then for any given target there would need to be only one code generator, and or only one interpreter. While feasible in principle this is not yet a standard mechanism.

One interesting by-product of the abstract machine approach is that computers have been subsequently built to execute the abstract machine code directly. These are hardware implementations of the 'Pcode' interpreter used for some versions of Pascal.

What then about the language in which the compiler

itself is written? The problem here is that there is a strongly held belief that 'systems' programs need a 'systems' language. One advantage of this belief is that the 'systems' language will be used by systems programmers and will be designed to handle a well defined set of problems.

Suppose what is required is a compiler for language X, and X is deemed unsuitable for writing this compiler. Then an available technique is to write the compiler for X in language Y, which is suitable. The language Y is itself not generally available so the compiler for Y is written in Y so that it can be compiled by a Y compiler wherever it may exist. If we have a Y compiler on machine A then we can write an X compiler to execute on machine A and generate code for machine A.

The Y compiler, written in Y, is transported to machine B by implementing new code generators for machine B. Now we have an X compiler which runs on machine B; unfortunately it still produces code for machine A. The code generators of the original compiler must then be modified to produce machine B code. Of course if the Y compiler and the X compiler had both been designed to produce output in the same abstract language, the work done to move Y from A to B will automatically produce a total move of the X compiler, since the abstract code to B translator had been written to move the Y compiler.

There is no way that the problem of producing code for the next machine can be overcome without some code being written specifically for the new machine.

In the foregoing, it was assumed that a Y compiler was available on some accessible real computer. If that is not the case then the process starts with the production of the first Y compiler. A further simplification of the whole process can be made if Y is the only language involved and it can itself be used to write portable applications programs.

Bootstrapping of compilers is done in various ways. The most straightforward is to write a simple compiler for a subset of the language in itself, i.e. the subset. At this stage there is no need to worry about efficiency of compiler or of compiled code. This compiler is then hand translated into whatever language is available and used to compile itself. The subset compiler is then improved to compile a more substantial portion of the target language but it is still written in the now compilable subset. The new compiler can now be compiled, preferably by the compiled version of the subset, simply to avoid perpetuating errors by failing to identify them early in the process. More improvements, using the richer language facilities now implemented, can be made and the process can continue interminably.

There is a technique for building up a program in layers to produce the initial Y compiler. As the intention of Y is that its compiler should be portable, it must not be written in the machine code of any particular computer. If there is no suitable language available which can be compiled, then a suitable compiler can be constructed in stages.

The approach is exemplified by the work of Waite, Pool and others.

In a series of papers the various levels of bootstrapping are defined. The layers are firstly SIMCMP. This is simple macro-processor. It is simple in two ways. First, it is simple to implement. Second, it is severely limited in the source code it accepts. However, it is written in FORTRAN and can be ported onto a new machine in a day or two. The FORTRAN logic has also been hand translated into BASIC and even Assembler. It is used to implement STAGE2, the second layer of the bootstrapping system.

STAGE2 is a much more powerful macro processor which can then be used to implement other programs. STAGE2 is coded in FLUB an assembler for an imaginary

special purpose computer. FLUB has 28 machine operations and two pseudo operations. The code body to
express each of these 30 macros must be written for each
new implementation. To produce an implementation of
STAGE2 requires an implementation of SIMCMP, the
implementation of the simple generated I/O interface and
the 30 macro expansions referred to above. Waite esti-
mates eight man hours for this task.

The portable C compiler

The transportability of UNIX depends heavily on the
portable C compiler. The original C compiler had been
used as a basis for the design of compilers for machines
other than the PDP/11. But there were problems and
incompatibilities, and the original compiler was not written with portability in mind. Accordingly a new compiler,
designed to be easily modified, was written. In each of the
various implementations about one quarter of the code –
in all about 8000 lines – is machine dependent. Machine
dependence is in two areas. The first is the simplest – the
code to produce language-dependent constructs, such as
function prologues and epilogues, which vary from
machine to machine, but are logically very much the same.
The difficult section is that involved in code generation
which requires an understanding both of C and of the
target hardware. The first pass of the compiler is largely
target machine-independent and the second pass then
generates the code for the target machine. The communication between the two compiler passes has allowed the
substitution of a FORTRAN 77 first pass which then
allows the various second passes originally designed for C
to produce machine code for the respective targets and so
provide FORTRAN 77 compilers. One additional advant-

age of the use of a largely portable compiler has been to reduce the maintenance problems and to retain compatibility between versions. The portable C system produces machine code for the target machine. This was deemed essential so that the translated program could be efficient. The inefficiency introduced by interpretation was felt to be intolerable.

Another, rather earlier, language designed with portability in mind is BCPL (Richards). The ideal of portability was incorporated both in the language whose facilities were designed to be largely portable, and in the design of the compiler itself. The problems as usual lie in the areas of arithmetic, character representation and operating system interface. Richards took the view that providing input and output facilities via library functions rather than as part of the language was better as the facilities could be implemented and/or enhanced with changing the compiler. The structure of the compiler has two passes communicating via an intermediate language. The second pass has its output 'Ocode', an abstract machine code. This in turn generated into the target machine code.

Bootstrapping BCPL involves writing a new code generator for Ocode. The distribution kit comprises a BCPL in BCPL compiler and an Ocode version. The process was simplified by compiling the compiler into INTCODE, which was specifically designed to make writing the code generator easy. Equally well of course an Ocode or INTCODE interpreter would be sufficient. Such a mechanism was used by Cowdenoy and Wallis (*Software P&E* vol. 12 no. 335) to transfer a PDP/11 Ocode version to a Z80 CP/M micro. This project involved writing an Ocode interpreter in Z80 code, a run-time support system to a loader. Incredibly the Ocode was transferred by typing in a script – some 50 000 key strokes. The paper regrettably does not indicate how many errors this introduced – nor how they were removed.

One strand that runs through the mechanisms of computer portability is the use of the order code of abstract machines. There was at one time the belief (and hope) that a universal abstract language could be defined. All translators would translate their source text into this language and each compiler would have a single translator from this language into its own machine code. The advantages would be immense. If we want compiler for M languages for N different computers, and if each compiler was to be written for each machine, then $M \times N$ compilers are needed. If each produces the same intermediate language only $M + N$ programs need writing.

However, this has not proved possible. The differences between machine instruction sets and the requirements of different languages are too great for a single intermediate language to be translated efficiently for all machines.

Nevertheless, this approach is a powerful one to implement and has resulted in the design of Pcode for Pascal and Ocode and INTCODE for BCPL. Waite and others have produced a more general intermediate language JANUS. Despite the overheads this technique is still attractive.

9

Available languages

9

Available languages

The previous chapter discussed of the mechanisms for compiler portability. Many projects do not justify the transportation of both the compiler and the application program itself and so in this chapter we look at the candidates that might be chosen for writing portable applications.

Compilers and assemblers are just tools. They take some textual representation or another and manipulate it according to some set of rules to another. Much heat has been generated over many years by the protagonists of one language or another claiming its superiority. The point at issue for writers of portable programs is whether or not the available tools are adequate for his requirements. It is useless to write programs in a language – however suitable – if the compiler can generate code for only one system. It is always open to an author to define yet another language and produce compilers for it. He need not in principle produce multiple compilers, but merely produce code for the various target machines on a single host. To transport applications code it is not necessary to transport the compilation system. Of course it may be simpler to use tools already implemented on a target system.

Obviously the portable program must be expressed in some computer language or other. Because machine independence is of the essence it follows that the program cannot be written in the machine code of a particular computer. Naturally enough this leads to the conclusion that a 'high-level' language should be chosen. However, before dismissing assemblers – as opposed to machine code – out of hand, it must be borne in mind that it is not essential that the target program is produced on the target machine. While there is a general assumption that portable programs must be capable of being supplied (in principle at least) in compilable form on each target, other mechanisms are feasible.

The assumption is that 'binary' versions are distributed only to provide a degree of protection from piracy. This is not necessarily the case. Macro-assemblers can be very powerful text manipulation tools and can be used to provide a translation process for codes other than the machine on which they run. Thus mechanisms can be devised where the portable code – or some section of it is written in a well defined set of macros and for each new machine the macro-expansions required are redefined and the program retranslated on the host. This of course presents the problem of transporting and testing the translated code.

In general however the usual approach adopted is to construct the bulk of the program in a high-level language available on the range of target machines. The implementor must therefore choose such a language at the outset. What criteria are used in such a decision? They will include:

1   Familiarity
2   Availability

3   Suitability
4   Standardization

There are many languages around. There are strongly held enthusiasms and preconceptions about all of them. However, a choice must be made. The implementor can choose either an existing language and use the existing compilers on his potential targets or he can decide to provide compilers for his targets.

If he chooses the former course he will have to make his choice from a relatively short list of candidates. These will include:

FORTRAN
ALGOL
COBOL
BASIC
Pascal
PL/I
BCPL
C
ADA

Standardization

At the end of list of criteria is 'Standardization'. This is a big problem for programmers. Languages in general use fall into two main categories; the first comprises those which are highly successful. These tend to be implemented on many machines and are thus widely available; they also tend to be 'extended'. Most of these extensions are highly desirable but are confined to a single implementation. Eventually a committee is set up and a standard is defined. Unfortunately pre-existing compilers do not conform to this standard. New compilers may conform initially but the temptation to 'improve' and extend the language is hard to resist.

Meanwhile the standards committee may be working on the new improved standard. In all likelihood the new language is better. Improvements are made both in programming techniques and specification techniques so that the new standard is a better definition of a language with better facilities, but is not the same language. Sometimes a language starts out as a development from a particular supplier of either hardware or software and the supplier then welcomes an externally applied standard to increase the acceptability of the product.

One important development is compiler verification. Because a language is, *de facto*, defined by its compilers, programs have been developed to verify the compiler. Such programs are written to check the correct compilation of programs without errors and the detection of known errors in others. Test data and example results are used to ensure the correctness of the generated code. Independent testing of both the syntax and semantics is useful because compiler writers do not attempt deliberately to be non-standard (excluding extensions). Nevertheless their syntax analysis and code generators are written to their own understanding of the language definition and it is therefore likely that in some areas each interpretation will be different. It is of assistance to everybody, compiler writers and users alike, that such independent testing takes place.

Another important development is program verification. This is also an extremely useful technique. A program verifier is a syntactic checker. It does not compile the program, but examines its syntax and structure. In general it does not verify algorithmic correctness. What it does seek to do is ensure first that the program conforms syntactically to a standard, and second that certain foolish

– but syntactically – legal errors are highlighted, using uninitialized variables, for example. The availability of such tools is likely then to influence choice of language, as there is a syntax check independent of any particular implementation.

The other main language category is the single vendor supplied product. It is not intended to imply that such products are not highly successful – some are. Indeed, because there is a single source of compilers, there is a better chance of syntactic and semantic consistency than is generally the case. There are examples in this field of both proprietary languages and of versions of 'standard languages'.

It is important for the writers of portable programs to realize that correctness of implementation is less important than consistency. Known problems can be overcome. What can cause problems is that programs which are well tried and tested sometimes no longer work or produce incorrect results when transferred to a new system.

One facility that is very attractive for implementing symbiotic systems is separate compilation of modules. If it is decided to isolate the potentially non-portable elements, then it is desirable to be able to ensure that the portable section remains unchanged. Separate compilation helps in this process.

FORTRAN

FORTRAN compilers are available on a wide range of computers and FORTRAN has been widely and successfully used for writing portable software. It is widely regarded as being rather crude and suitable only for 'scientific programs'. This is certainly not so; it has been used quite successfully for programs of all types and even 'scientific' programs will nowadays try to achieve 'user-friendliness' and a high degree of data validation, neither of which are the attributes of traditional scientific programs. The charge of crudity is levelled mainly at its structural deficiences and its control statements. Certainly more modern languages have more elegant mechanisms. One approach to FORTRAN usage that can be considered is 'RATFOR'. RATFOR is a preprocessor which takes as input an extended version of FORTRAN with better structural features and translates these additional features into regular FORTRAN, which can then be compiled in the usual way. It is a mechanism not so much for avoiding machine dependencies but for improving the acceptability of FORTRAN as a programming language. FORTRAN is defined by an ANSI committee. There are two versions of what is still called FORTRAN and in addition a new standard known as FORTRAN 77. This new standard addresses certain known deficiencies and problems, but the new language is not entirely compatible with the old.

FORTRAN has always supported separate compilation and there is usually a library mechanism to support the load module/link-editing phase.

The particular problems of FORTRAN are to be found in character handling and in direct-access input/output. There are wide variations in both the syntactic representation of characters within FORTRAN programs and the mechanisms for accessing non-sequential files. FORTRAN because of its wide availability, has been subjected to much analysis and there is an entire book concerned with identifying and defining a sub-set 'Compatible FORTRAN' and a recently produced book describing how to write FORTRAN in a portable manner.

The cited papers on RATFOR and BASIC contain interesting commentaries on the FORTRAN language.

PL/I

This language was designed and implemented by IBM. It is a language with a very wide range of facilities and was intended to be applicable to the entire spectrum of programming problems. It has features most easily implemented on IBM style hardware and software. Compilers for it are large and difficult to write. It has not been used widely outside the IBM world and is not an obvious candidate for portable programs.

ADA

The US Department of Defense (DOD) decided that for the programming of 'embedded' systems the cost of programming and program maintenance could be reduced by adopting one language throughout. Accordingly a specification of requirements was produced. Four competing teams produced language specifications and the winner was named ADA. As well as the language the design project now included the definition of a support environment. The goal is obviously very desirable.

The language includes some novel features and doubts have been expressed that perhaps they are too novel. Compilers are becoming available – at this stage for subsets – which are strictly not allowed. The European Commission is also supporting the language. It is likely then to be widely available. It is too new to be chosen for portable programs at this stage.

ALGOL

There are several languages called ALGOL. ALGOL 60 was one of the first attempts at a rigorous description of an algorithmic representation language. It was a highly successful effort and introduced new and powerful constructs. It suffers from the main disadvantages that it is defined in terms of a rich character set and there has been no *de facto* standard for its representation in a more realistic set of characters. It also neatly avoids specifying input/output mechanisms. The problems that arise in implementing its highly sophisticated recursion and parameter mechanisms tend to produce programs that are slower and larger than produced by other languages. ALGOL is not universally available and there are large differences in the facilities provided by different compilers.

The absence of built-in input/output facilities can be seen as an advantage. The user is obliged to consider his requirements and is then able to design and implement the necessary procedures. These can be re-implemented for each target. The advantage is that he knows what he has to do.

COBOL

It is always assumed that COBOL is the best (or only) language for the writing of commercial programs. It is defined as an American Standard. The document defining COBOL '74 is about 1.5″ (35mm) thick. The problem is that the range of options defined in the specification is very large.

A language to qualify as 'COBOL' has only to include three of these many options. For whatever reason the literature in COBOL portability is thin on the ground.

One trend that has emerged is the provision of portable subset compilers. A manufacturer produces a compiler for his own definition of COBOL and then makes this compiler available on various machines. Thus the programmer can write programs to transport to machines with such support. There are several such systems now available. There is no implication that these are not 'proper' subsets, but the use of a 'standard' subset as implemented will improve the chances of portability.

Single supplier COBOL compilers are available for a variety of systems, and the use of these standards may help towards portability amongst those systems with such compilers.

BASIC

This language was originally designed for an early time-sharing system. It is widely available on microcomputers, often being the only available language and implemented in ROM. It is usually interpreted, though some compilers are becoming available. Its original design was very simple and it lacks many features which are now regarded as desirable. For example it lacks parameters in its subroutine calls. It has no program structuring features. However, there is a lot of it about. The variations between dialects are considerable, especially in character handling and I/O. Many versions do not implement integers variables requiring all numbers to be floating point. The basic specification allows only single character names. In general it is not a desirable language for portable programs.

There are various 'standard' but incompatible BASICs available and implemented on several different micros. The problem is that some of the smaller machines, and of course there are more of these than large ones, thus representing a larger market, may support only BASIC which puts the writer of portable programs in a dilemma.

C

C was originally the language of UNIX and was used both for the implementation of UNIX and as the principal programming language under it. Many compilers are now available for other systems. The language is strongly typed and was designed originally, and subsequently refined, with portability in mind. It has a variety of features included to aid portability. The I/O facilities are designed to be consistently implemented on various machines. Two particularly powerful features are the ability to 'include' files and a conditional preprocessor which contains a limited string substitution facility. These two features, if used sensibly, are a significant aid to portability. It must be stressed that they do not of themselves solve the problem of transporting programs. They provide mechanisms to allow solutions to the problems of differences between systems to be more readily incorporated into program texts. The programmer must still identify differences and provide solutions himself.

Most C systems support separate compilation of modules and provide extensive libraries for inclusion at loading. This is a considerable advantage in creating versions of a system. The type checking is difficult to achieve across separate compilations.

C has an ingenious approach to the problem of 'pointers', which are, crudely, machine addresses. As the address space of computers has grown it is no longer always possible to represent these addresses as a single integer. Accordingly C introduces a new type guaranteed to be big enough to hold a pointer, the size depending on the computer in question. This allows a consistent approach to pointer handling. Unfortunately not all modern hardware has a suitably simple method of representing long addresses and so address manipulation mechanisms will be different on different systems.

Another advantage of C is the idea of standard libraries. These are part of the *de facto* standards adopted by many of the available systems. Included in such libraries are standard I/O facilities and character and string manipulating routines. If these are used consistently and implemented correctly, they are of great assistance in producing portable programs. They do not however solve all the problems that occur when something non-standard in the underlying system must be coped with. Screen handling is a good example of this sort of problem.

One problem with C is that it is possible to write programs of some considerable opacity, it has a syntax which is powerful but rather dense. This feature has reduced its acceptability. It is also possible to use C almost as a high-level assembly language, the result of which is no aid to portability.

Work is in hand on producing C standards. Current implementations tend to be 'Kernighan and Ritchie'-compatible with extensions. Even with different 'K&R' implementations under MS/DOS there are differences in the effect of 'standard' character input routines. Two different, but equally good, MS/DOS implementations use the same named 'include' file for accessing DOS functions. Though the files have the same name, and the compilers run on the same system, the mechanisms supported are incompatible. Converting programs using such features to run on UNIX systems shows yet more idiosyncrasies.

10

Software tools

10

Software tools

Languages and macroprocessors are tools, but they are not the only tools available. Other tools can be used, and the more the process of program text manipulation can be automated and mechanized the less clerical errors will occur. The available tools fall into several classes. There are general purpose text-manipulative programs. These include text-editors and macroprocessors. There are language-specific text manipulators, such as Wootton, Jeffreys and Partners GENERATOR program, RATFOR, PFORT, PBASIC and Lint.

The last three are language syntax checkers. The principle on which verifiers is based is as follows. It can (and probably must) be assumed that the available compilers will do an adequate job compiling syntactically correct programs written in a standard version of their target language. Many of the problems of different compilers disappear if they are relied on only to translate correct programs written to conform strictly to the standard. The potential inconsistency problems are minimized as the syntactic extensions are not used; nor is the error detection mechanism invoked. After all if a program is being transported it is reasonable to assume that it is syntactically and semantically correct on at least one system. So the idea is to use a verifier to ensure conformity. A verifier does not compile programs but seeks to ensure that they conform to a standard language syntax. It can be extended to check other possible areas of error. The sort of additional checks that can be made include looking for the use of uninitialized variables in expressions, and for sections of code that can never be executed. It is possible to check for type mismatches which the compiler (correctly) accepts, but which are unintentional. The detection of the use of uninitialized variables is of particular importance as systems vary widely in how they cope with uninitialized storage. Some may set it to zero, some to an identifiable illegal value and others make no effort to change the unpredictable values left by some previous program. Thus a program which has always worked previously because uninitialized variables have been set to zero may well fail where this is not the case. There are compilers which will detect and report an error if there are code sections which cannot be reached and thus cannot be executed. Certain errors in the program may be masked in some systems because they happen to corrupt program areas never in fact utilized. The verifiers mentioned are PFORT, for FORTRAN, PBASIC for BASIC and Lint which 'picks the fluff off C'.

RATFOR is a FORTRAN preprocessor. The principle behind RATFOR is that, while FORTRAN has deficiencies, it is widely available and so why not create mechanisms to use it better? RATFOR then has extended facilities and improvements in textual layout, a wider character set and improved facilities for comments. Note that none of these of themselves improve portability. It adds desirable control structures to FORTRAN which can themselves be described in FORTRAN and translates into syntactically correct FORTRAN mechanically. It illustrates a basic principle of using what is available as elegantly and as economically as possible. It is much easier and much more portable to 'preprocess' into a widely available language than it is to produce new compilers. RATFOR is itself written in a 'portable' FORTRAN. There is no need to transport the preprocessor if its output is readily available, and can be transported.

A refinement to the use of RATFOR is to include a macroprocessor in the sequence of operations. Thus the program text is written to include macro-definitions of those items identified to be machine- or system-dependent. A macroprocessor with the macro-expansions designed for the particular target system is used to produce a RATFOR text.

RATFOR has been extensively used to the extent that there are papers discussing the improvement of its implementation to reduce (very significantly) the cost of its use in machine resource terms.

Portable file systems

In the discussion on emulation techniques (Chapter 6) the idea of a bounce library was introduced. A 'bounce' package accepts calls of one format and translates them into calls of another, appropriate to the current host machine. The STRESS implementation uses this idea by providing a subroutine with standard calls which are mapped into the appropriate actions for each host computer.

In a paper by Hanson (*SP&E* 10/8/623) a mechanism is discussed for providing a portable file directory system (PDS). As discussed in Chapter 3 on software problems, every operating system has its own idiosyncratic approach to the organization of files. The approach of Multics,

UNIX, Primos, MUSIC-11 and others which seems to have desirable characteristics is a system of hierarchical directories. Such directories are implemented in later versions of MS/DOS. In such a file organization there exists a master file directory (MFD), either one for the entire system or one for each logical or physical disc. There are practical advantages in having at least one MFD associated with each removable disc pack.

Entries in a file directory are either files or further directories. Directories are of course just files, but should be handled by the system rather than by applications programs.

Conventionally the entries in the MFD are all user file directory (UFD) entries. Each UFD then can contain entries that are either user files or further UFDs, sometimes called sub-UFDs. Any file in the system can then be referred to by a 'tree' or path name, consisting of a list of the directories descending from the MFD followed by the name of the file itself. It should be noted that nothing in the outlined scheme has been implied about either the file-naming conventions nor the nature of the files themselves.

The implementation of such a scheme will, of course, impose conventions. In an operating system implementation one datum associated with each file name will be a pointer of some sort to the physical position on disc of the data in the file. In Hanson's system this data entry is the local file name, i.e. the PDS maps into the local file conventions. One UNIX extension to the basic hierarchical structure implemented in the PDS is the concept of linking, that is to say establishing an alias for a file so that it can be referenced by more than one tree name. Another useful concept in a tree-structured directory system is that of the current or attached UFD. At any given time one particular directory is the current directory. This can be further refined by specifying a 'home' directory and providing a mechanism for returning 'home'.

Hanson's PDS is implemented with a small set of primitives. These are:

mkfile (tree, host-name) which associates a tree name with an existing host file name.

mkdir (tree) which creates a directory

chain (tree) which sets the current directory

link (tree1. tree2) creates a link

unlink (tree) removes a link. The removal of the last link effectively removes the entry.

openf (tree,mode) which opens a file. Mode is passed untouched to the host routine. *Openf* returns a machine dependent value to be used in subsequent I/O operations.

creatf (tree, mode) generates a new file and then opens it. It uses an option of *mkfile*, which, if called without a host name, generates a unique host name.

Hanson stresses the importance of the transparency of the mode specified in *openf* and *creatf*. He believes the usefulness of his PDS would be affected adversely by changes that required it to be aware of I/O transfers. As the range of possibilities for mode varies widely between systems on each, there is here a problem for applications portability. Some systems for example will create a new file for writing if one is opened which did not previously exist. There is a case for including in a portable file system mechanisms for consistency, even at the cost of some overhead.

Hanson's PDS is implemented in RATFOR in about 680 lines of code. The data structure to support the PDS is a single file containing lines of ASCII text, one for each file. These lines contain: file type, number of links, creation time and date, most recent access time and date, host system name.

A directory is a file of lines each of which comprises a PDS name and a number which is an index to the one file containing the file description lines. The reason for holding the data as text is for ease of portability.

The implementation details are described in the paper, as are some conclusions drawn from its use and a discussion of the limitations of its implementation. It has been used successfully and is an interesting approach to solving what can be an important source of problems in portability. Any inefficiencies introduced are relatively unimportant as directory manipulations are performed much less often than I/O operations. There is a strong case for providing a portable I/O system as well as a portable directory system. If the host-operating system provides a good set of I/O operations, then the mapping from the portable set will be easy and therefore cheap in terms of efficiency. If the host is deficient, then by providing a portable system with a good set of facilities, the applications programming task is simplified and the code needs writing only once for each host.

There is a growing trend towards device-independent I/O mechanisms and in general this is desirable. However, there are certain operations where a degree of device specificity is necessary. I/O which consists of a stream of characters can be device-independent, but certain operations, on say, the user terminal or intermediate disc files are of their nature specific to at least a class of devices. However, these desirable features can be defined and implemented in a portable manner. Some file systems have superimposed a fixed size blocking structure while others allow the user to treat a file as a contiguous string of bytes with a logical pointer which can be positioned anywhere between the beginning and end of file. This latter approach allows an applications program to avoid the problems of buffer handling and allows the choice of record characteristics to be based on algorithmic need, rather than have them imposed by the system.

By defining primitives to allow such logical positioning and the reading/writing of arbitrary numbers of bytes, these facilities can be provided in a portable manner.

Similarly a set of terminal driving primitives could be defined and implemented portably for each different terminal type supported.

The additional overheads might well be less than those incurred by the language's own I/O system.

GENERATOR

This is Wootton, Jeffrey and Partners' program maintenance tool. It was developed specifically for the maintenance of portable FORTRAN programs. It is axiomatic that there should only be one master version of the code of a program. GENERATOR's job is to process the master code text to produce separate versions for each target machine. While GENERATOR is itself written in FORTRAN, it is intended to produce machine-specific versions of a portable program, rather than be portable itself.

The principle facilities of GENERATOR are:

1 The insertion of common declarations
2 Optional inclusion of text
3 String substitutions

There is maintained a compact source code file and each run of GENERATOR takes a set of parameters to direct its action. The mechanism used is to embed in the text 'G cards' i.e. cards with a 'G' in column 1. This distinguishes them from FORTRAN source which must have a C, a digit or a blank in the first column. G cards are free format with blanks or '/' slashes ignored or used as delimiters. The compilable output is created from the compact source file by including some card images and omitting others.

G cards may themselves be included in the output file, with the G changed to a C. Such cards are said to have been commented.

The compact source is made of 'decks', which may be either common or code decks. These are signalled by a deck card which defines it as common or code and gives it a four-character name.

Within decks there may be:

1 I cards. These control the insertion of common decks into code decks.
2 A cards. These control the conditional inclusion of cards. The mechanism allows the nesting of conditions within a hierarchy of levels and the 'anding' or 'oring' of conditions.
3 Other cards to control commenting and string substitution.

GENERATOR does not in itself provide any portability features. What it does do is provide text manipulation facilities to aid the maintenance of a single copy of the source of a program while providing different machine versions. It is still necessary to write the system-dependent code.

11

The present situation

11

The present situation

Much of the analysis in this book is of relatively old work. Surely by now the problem should have been solved. However, it has not.

The problem may have been perpetuated by the widespread use of IBM pcs and the various 'clones'. This has created a vast market for software which does not have to be portable, for all the hosts are perceived to be the same. It isn't in practice quite like that as the differences between 'compatible' machines are sometimes enough to ensure lack of portability. The appearance of standardization may have been enough to reduce the effort put into portability.

It is widely believed that C is the answer. In a prevoius chapter on languages (Chapter 9) some of the pitfalls were alluded to. There is a vast range of C compilers available for PC/DOS and MS/DOS. There are differences in implementation and between the function libraries provided. A frequent need is the input of a single nonprinting character without echo to the screen and without the need to push the return button, for example a cursor or function key. In two versions of C under MS/DOS, both respected and effective compilers, this function is provided inconsistently. Each provides a mechanism for making calls to the underlying operating system, which would allow the user to implement such a function himself, but the two mechanisms are different. One of those compilers comes with an excellent 'portable' editor provided in source form. Conditional compilation allows the editor to be compiled and run on various different operating systems. In the case of MS/DOS keys are read directly. In another operating system, this same simple action takes a page of C code. However the second compiler could not be used to compile the MS/DOS code unchanged! Even the keenest protagonists of C admit it is possible to produce highly machine-specific programs. Moreover the very power and freedom of expression that C permits is one reason it is not used more widely. Its reputation as a 'hacker's' language does not endear it to all, and many of its features fly in the face of current thinking about security within languages. However it is becoming widely available on operating systems other than UNIX.

UNIX is itself suggested as the route forward to truly portable software. This has not yet been shown to be so. There are two major reasons for this. The first is that UNIX is provided by a wide variety of suppliers and implementors and this has inevitably led to inconsistency. Second, it has vociferous critics who deny its universal applicability and so quite a lot of software is not available for it. Efforts are being made to standardize the system and extend it consistently into those areas where it is felt to be deficient. Those efforts are sufficient proof that care must still be taken.

The other current trend, if we can ignore for the time being expert systems, is 4GLs and application generators. These products attack another problem area altogether. Their goal is to simplify and accelerate the production of useful programs. It could perhaps be argued that this will reduce the need for portable programs, as the value of the program will be reduced.

However, they are in themselves strictly irrelevant in the search for portability. Their designers could, if they so chose, ensure that they were capable of producing programs that were portable, but that is exactly the same problem as with any other program translating tool.

12

Summary and conclusions

12
Summary and conclusions

There has been a lot of effort over the past 20 years to crack
the problem of program portability. The problem still
remains. It is not yet the case in general that programs
written in a high-level language will run unchanged on
another system with another compiler for the same language. If the language has been chosen carefully and much
effort has been taken both in the coding and the algorithmic design, then there is a chance that it may work and an
excellent chance that the changes will need to be made
only to certain predefined subroutines.

The main hope of achieving simple portability lies in the
greater availability of standard operating systems. At the
moment there is a growth in the use and supply of
hardware manufacturer-independent operating systems –
but mostly on micro systems. There are independent
systems supported on some minis, but these are usually
alternatives to the manufacturer's own system. There does
not appear to be any trend to a universal order code, each
manufacturer still producing his own idiosyncratic
instruction set.

These independent systems are sometimes transported

by several groups and this is likely to produce a lack of consistency between offerings of the same order of magnitude as the differences between different compilers of the same language, even for the same computer.

This is probably inevitable and perhaps it has its positive aspects. No one system or architecture is perfect, or at least none is recognized as such. In the continually changing field of the manufacture and use of computers, at least some of the changes are improvements and some are significant breakthroughs. The growing provision of emulator hardware and downwards-compatible systems gives hope that progress can be made without the expense of rewriting or totally discarding all that has gone before.

There is a growing trend for manufacturers of systems to be less insecure and less defensive and to look to independent suppliers for more and more of the software provided. The imperative to be the total system supplier is weakening, and this must be a trend which benefits the user.

Often a user will have greater problems because his data are kept in such a way that a particular program, or suite of programs, is needed to process them. Increasingly packages are available to perform most standard data processing functions on most systems. However, he may be trapped by having both his data and his working methods tied to a system which can neither be moved to better or cheaper hardware, nor economically enhanced to provide more facilities. He can expect his original supplier now to provide a compatible upgrade path, or for the competition to exploit a weakness and offer an effective alternative. Nevertheless, the problem of upgrading should be faced right from the start and his plans based on an appreciation of the likely hardware trends and of the need to be able to exploit his software investment for the foreseeable future.

There is one interesting factor in the equation which is largely missing, and that is the design of order codes.

These tend to be vastly different and usually regarded by software writers more as a challenge than an opportunity. There appears to be little coordination of the hardware/ software requirements. A few manufacturers are embedding operating systems facilities 'in silicon', but unless they make the right decisions, that will inhibit the growth of better software. Software writers tend in general to accept the hardware and find more or less elegant ways to live with it rather than seek to change it.

For suppliers of software the three possible approaches outlined earlier remain. There are examples to be found of each in practice.

Each allows a different mechanism for portability and requires different skills and levels of investment. Though the ground-up approach is the most complete and the achievement of total portability of 'applications' code is possible, it requires the employment of skills additional to, and different from, those needed for the applications areas. In particular, it needs the skills to comprehend fully each new architecture and I/O structure, and to design code generators or interpreters exactly to mimic the semantics achieved on the earlier machines. There is a high level of investment required as this is a non-trivial task and extensive design and testing has to be undertaken. When successful, the system will be compatible with, and programs transferable between, any other manifestations of itself. The investment will only be worthwhile if the whole system is sufficiently attractive and well supported for its use to become widespread. There will still be the problem of interchanging applications written under this particular regime with any others, in both directions.

There is a strong case for combining this approach with elements of the 'accommodating hosts' so that more software is available and the attractions of the system thereby enhanced. 'Accommodating hosts' are an attractive mechanism for moving existing software into more powerful or cheaper, or indeed both, environments. If the hardware is different then the approach is not dissimilar to the 'symbiotic' approach, except that some of the algorithmic effort is by the systems implementor, rather than the applications programmer. 'Accommodating host' systems are only justifiable if there is a large amount of software worth transferring and a large market interested in using additional facilities while retaining existing programs.

Both these approaches are relatively expensive and potentially require a major change by existing users if sold into existing markets. For the development of new market areas, they are well justified as it will be possible – if not easy – to take advantage of new hardware as it appears and retain the investment made in application packages.

The least expensive option is the 'symbiotic' approach. If it is done well, the market for the product should be almost unlimited, as the program can be transported to most environments economically. Programs of this class exist and are successful technically in their transportability.

For the programmer deciding to produce a 'symbiotic' portable program there are some big decisions to be taken at the very earliest design stage. The first decision to be made is the programming language to be used. Despite its considerable drawbacks, and despite the obloquy heaped upon it, FORTRAN emerges as a very strong contender. It has been used successfully in many projects. Tools to improve its use and ensure compatibility are available and there are examples of its successful use as both a systems language and for commercial programs as well as its traditional use for scientific programming It is very widely available and its deficiencies and the areas where problems can arise are well understood and described. No doubt it would be better if some other language were as widely available. Pascal is now giving a good run for its money and experience is being gained in its use for portable projects. There are differences of implementation between Pascal compilers, but there are also available transported implementations of the same compiler.

C has emerged as a strong contender. However C compilers are more likely to be available on more modern systems, indeed on some there is a confusing choice of competing systems. Clearly their authors and their sellers would argue that they are not all the same.

Of the less well known languages BCPL compilers have been produced for many computers.

If the aim of the designer is to produce programs available across the board, then he is forced to consider FORTRAN (old style at that) very seriously. Despite the criticisms of the language philosophy and design from some quarters, the ADA bandwaggon, fuelled by the DOD and the European Commission, will undoubtedly roll. At this stage in its development and implementation it is too early to know where the problems will lie.

Whichever language is finally chosen, the designer will have to produce for himself a minimum set of requirements from his operating systems and provide machine-dependent routines with machine-independent interfaces to support them. Except for a single product line, it will probably pay dividends to implement a file and an I/O environment to free the applications programmer from the idiosyncrasies of each host. Above all else he must enforce and obey his own restrictions and standards. It will probably be worth the investment in syntactic verifiers to minimize the risks of failing to do this.

It is hard enough to write correct programs in one environment – it requires insight and discipline for it to work correctly on many.

Further reading

The books and articles cited are divided into sections corresponding with the chapters of the book. It must be stressed that some of the citied works encompass more than a single topic. In particular some of the work on compiler portability presents ideas and techniques applicable to transporting other classes of program.

Software Practice and Experience is published by John Wiley and I make no apologies for the fact that there are many articles cited from this publication. It publishes many excellent papers emphasizing practical experience catering particularly for the writers of software, using the traditional definition of software. I have also cited *Computer Journal* which is the British Computer Society's journal.

Books

Brown, P.J. (ed.), *Software Portability – An advanced course*, CUP, 1977.

This book is a collection of papers presented at a course in 1977. It offers a wide view of the subject; some of the material is still of interest.

Dahlstrand, I., *Software Portability and Standards*, Ellis Horwood, 1984.

Interesting discussion of the problems encountered by the author in implementing systems.

Frank, W.L., *Critical Issues in Software*, Wiley Interscience, 1983.

A fascinating discussion of many of the non-technical issues in software.

Godfrey, M.D., et al, *Machine-Independent Organic Software Tools (MINT)*, Academic Press, 1985.

A description of a complete ground-up implementation of a 'virtual machine' system and tool set.

Muxworthy, D.T. (ed.), *Programming for Software Sharing*, D. Reidel Publishing Co., 1983.

A collection of interesting papers, not all of them directly relevant.

Lecarme, O. and Gart, M.P., *Software Portability*, McGraw-Hill, 1986.

A useful analysis of the problems. The solutions presented are from the fields of systems software.

Wallis, P.J.L., *Portable Programming*, Macmillan, 1982.
This book reviews a wide range of techniques.

X/OPEN Portability Guide, Elsevier Science Publishers B.V., 1985.

A set of guidelines and intentions from a cooperating group of manufacturers attempting to set and implement a joint standard.

Articles

Hamlet, R.G., and Haralick, R.H., 'Transportable Package Software', *Software Practice and Experience*, 10, p. 1009, 1980.

Lemoine, M., and Muller, J., 'Software Transferability – A practical approach', *Software Practice and Experience*, 11, p. 425, 1981.

Waite, W.M., 'Hints on Distributing Portable Software', *Software Practice and Experience*, 5, p. 295, 1975.

Hardware
'An Implementation Guide to a Proposed Standard for Floating Point Arithmetic', *IEEE Computer*, p. 69, 1980.

Thimbleby, H., 'The Design of a Terminal Independent Package', *Software Practice and Experience*, 17(5), p. 351, 1987.

Yip, C.K., 'The Pascal Graphics System', *Software Practice and Experience*, 14(2), p. 101, 1984.

Ground-up
Johnson and Ritchie, 'Portability of C Programs and the Unix System', *Bell System Technical Journal*, 57(6), 1978.

Kernighan, B.W., and Mashey, J.R., 'The Unix Programming Environment', *Software Practice and Experience*, 9(1), p. 1, 1979.

Perkins, D.R., and Volper, D., 'UCSD Pascal on the Vax, Portability and Performance', *Software Practice and Experience*, 14(5), p. 473, 1984.

Zwanepoel, W., and Lantz, K.A., 'Perseus; retrospective on a Portable Operating System', *Software Practice and Experience*, 14, p. 31, 1984.

Microprocessors
'A Platform for True Program Portability with Examples from Micro Cobol'. *Proceedings 4th International Software Engineering Conference*, Munich, p. 332, September 1979.

Irvine, 'UCSD System makes Programs Portable, *Electric Design*, August 1980.

Powell, H.S., 'Experience of Transporting and Using the SOLO Operating System', *Software Practice and Experience*, 9, p. 561, 1979.

Theaker, C.J., and Frank, G.R., 'MUSS – A Portable Operating System', *Software Practice and Experience*, 9, p. 633, 1979.

Symbiosis
Alcock and Shearing, 'GENESYS', *Structural Engineer*, April 1970.

Ford, B., Bartley, J., Due Croz, J., and Hague, S.J., 'The NAG Library Machine', *Software Practice and Experience*, 9, p. 65, 1979.

Hague, S., and Ford, B., 'Portability, Prediction & Correction', *Software Practice and Experience*, 6, p. 61, 1976.

Linnainmaa, S., 'Ice Cream , Transportable Software for Creating Friendly Human Interfaces', *Software Practice and Experience*, 16(8), p. 739, 1986.

Richardson, C., and Hague, S., 'Design & Implementation of the NAG Master Library File System', *Software Practice and Experience*, 7, p. 127, 1977.

Saxena, S., and Field, J.A., 'Portable Real-Time Software for 8-bit microprocessors', *Software Practice and Experience*, 15(3), p. 277, 1985.

Shearing and Alcock, 'GENTRAN', *Proceedings Colloque International Seminar, les Systems Integrés*, Genie Civil Liège, 1972.

Languages

FORTRAN

Alcock, C., *Illustrating Fortran*, Cambridge University Press, 1982.

Day, A.C., *Compatible Fortran*, Cambridge University Press, 1978.

Knuth, D.E., 'An Empirical Study of Fortran Programs', *Software Practice and Experience*, 6, p. 105, 1971.

Larmouth, J., 'Serious Fortran', *Software Practice and Experience*, 3, p. 87, 1973.

Larmouth, J., 'Fortran 77, Portability', *Software Practice and Experience*, 11, p. 1071, 1981.

Onibere, E.A., 'Writing Portable Fortran Programs for Microcomputers', *Software Practice and Experience*, 15 (4), p. 321, 1985.

COBOL

Triance, J.M., 'Portable Programming in Cobol, Infotech State of the Art', *Report on Life-Cycle Maintenance*, 1980.

Triance, J.M., 'A Study of Cobol Portability', *Computer Journal*, 21, p. 278, 1978.

ADA

Ardo, A., 'Experience Acquiring and Re-Targeting a Portable Ada Compiler', *Software Practice and Experience*, 17(4), p. 291, 1987.

Ibsen, L., 'A Portable Virtual Machine for Ada', *Software Practice and Experience*, 14(1), p. 17, 1984.

Wichmann, B., et al, 'Ada Europe Guidelines for the Portability of Ada Programs', *NPL Report* DNACS 52/81.

BCPL

Richards, Whitby & Stevens, *BCPL The Language and its Compiler*, Cambridge University Press, 1979.

RTL/2

Barnes, J.G.P., 'The Standardisation of RTL/2', *Software Practice and Experience*, 10, p. 707, 1980.

General language use

'The preparation of Guidelines for Portable Programming in High Level Languages', *Computer Journal*, 82, p. 375.

Tools

Brown, P.J., 'SUPERMAC, A Macro Facility that can be Added to Existing Compilers', *Software Practice and Experience*, 10, p. 431, 1980.

Brown, P.J., *Macro Processors and Techniques for Portable Software*, Wiley, 1974.

Comer, 'Mouse 4: An Improved Implementation for the RATFOR Preprocessor', *Software Practice and Experience*, 8, p. 35, 1978.

Doyle, J.K and Mandelberg, K.I., 'A Portable PDP-11 Simulator', *Software Practice and Experience*, 14(11), p. 1047, 1984.

Hopkins, T.R., 'PBASIC, A Verifier for Basic', *Software Practice and Experience*, 10, p. 175, 1980.

Kernighan, B.W., and Plauger, G., *Software Tools*, Addison Wesley, 1976.

Kernighan, B.W., 'RATFOR, A Preprocessor for a Rational Fortran', *Software Practice and Experience*, 5, p. 395, 1975.

Lawrence, 'SCRUB, Systematically Clean and Remember Users BASIC', *Software Practice and Experience*, 8, p. 227, 1978.

Munn, R.J., and Stewart, J.H., 'RATMAC; A Preprocessor for Writing Portable Scientific Software', *Software Practice and Experience*, 10, p. 743, 1980.

Ryder, B.G., *The PFORT Verifier*, 4, p. 359, 1974.

Snow, 'The Software Tools Project', *Software Practice and Experience*, 8, p. 585, 1978.

Steffen, J.L., 'Experience with a Portable Debugging Tool', *Software Practice and Experience*, 14(4), p. 323, 1984.

Compiler portability and macro systems

Cowderoy R.I., and Wallis, P.J.L., 'The Transfer of a BCPL Compiler to the Z80 Microcomputer', *Software Practice and Experience*, 12, p. 235, 1982.

Hadden and Waite, 'Experience with the Universal Intermediate Language, Janus', *Software Practice and Experience*, 8, p. 601, 1978.

Hughes, J.G., and Connolly, M., 'A Portable Implementation of a Modular Multi-processing Database Programming Language', *Software Practice and Experience*, 17(8), p533, 1987.

Lakos, C.A., 'Implementing BCPL on the Burroughs, B6700', *Software Practice and Experience*, 10, p. 673, 1980.

Orgass and Waite, 'A base for a mobile programming system', *CACM* 12(9), p. 507, 1969.

Richards, M., 'The Portability of the BCPL Compiler', *Software Practice and Experience*, 1, p. 135, 1971.

Waite, W.H., 'Building a Mobile Programming System', *Computer Journal* 13, p. 28, 1970.

Waite, 'A Language Independent Macro Processor', *CACM* 10(7), p. 433, 1967.

Waite, 'The Mobile Programming System, STAGE 2', *CACM* 13 (7), p. 415, 1970.

Index

directories 124
DISKIO 85

EBCDIC 17
emulation
    advantages 71–2
    aim 71
    hardware mechanisms 22,
        72–4
    order code 77–9
    software mechanisms 74–9

floppy discs and portability 36,
    37
FLUB 98–9
FORTRAN
    applications 109–110
    portability 7, 28, 85–6, 138
FORTRAN (77) 87–8, 99, 110

GENERATOR 86, 125–6
GENESYS 43

hardware emulation 22

I/O (Input/Output) mechanisms
    23–4, 124–5

JANUS 101

Lint 119, 120

magnetic tape, and portability
    36
master file directories (MFDs)
    122
Micro COBOL 64–7
MS/DOS 64
MUSIC-II 76, 122

Ocode 100, 101
Onyx system, and UNIX 63–4
operating systems
    functions 33–4
    and named files 34–6
    portability 8–9, 58–9, 135

operating systems (*continued*)
    purpose 33
    variety 32–3
order codes, extensions 22–3

packages, portability 9
Pascal 138–9
PBASIC 119, 120
PC/DOS 64
PFORT 119, 120
PL/1 111
portability
    accommodating host systems
        137–8
        examples 42
    benefits 4–5
    consistency 109
    definition 7–8
    design for 41–2
        examples 42
    file systems 121–4
    and floppy discs 36
    ground-up systems
        examples 42, 43, 55–67
        problems 45
    languages 107–15
    and magnetic tape 36
    operating systems 8–9, 58–9
    and program speed 9
    symbiotic systems
        arithmetic facilities 46–7
        character representation
            47–8
        examples 42, 83–9
        I/O facilities 50–1
        implementation language
            45–6, 138–9
        program and data space
            49–50
    and terminals 36–7, 38
    trends 130–1, 135–9
    verification 51
programming languages
    standards 29
    syntax 28–9
programs
    emulation 74–9